THE

PRESSURE

PARADOX™

(A COMPANION TO THE HABIT FACTOR)

YOUR PATH TO MAXIMUM PRODUCTIVITY, PERFORMANCE & PEACE OF MIND

◆

~ KILL PROCRASTINATION
INCREASE EFFECTIVENESS
MANAGE STRESS & ANXIETY. ~

MARTIN GRUNBURG

EQUILIBRIUM ENTERPRISES, INC.

Disclaimer: The advice and strategies contained herein may not be suitable for every individual or situation. This work is sold with the understanding that the Author and Publisher are not engaged in rendering any legal, accounting, health or other professional services. Neither the Author nor Publisher shall be held liable for any damages arising either directly or indirectly here from.

Library of Congress Cataloging-in-Publication data is available upon request.
ISBN: 978-0-9820501-8-7   0-9820501-8-6
Grunburg, Martin A.
The Pressure Paradox™ – *Your Path to Maximum Productivity, Performance & Peace of Mind.*

First Edition: October, 2015
Printed in the United States

Get The Habit Factor® on Audible

FREE Audiobook Chapters of this book!

*Expected availability December 2015!

Become a NEW Audible.com listener, and when The Habit Factor® is your FIRST title please email: Sales AT equilibrium-ent.com with receipt for 1yr Subscription to ProCloud app! (iOS only)

Subscribe Today to the top-ranked "**Habits 2 Goals**" **Podcast**: iTunes or Android.

Cover Design: Equilibrium Enterprises, Inc.

Volume discounts for non-profit, educational, business and promotional use are available. Ask about the custom imprinted book-jacket service with your organization's logo. For bulk sales information, please email: **booksales@equilibrium-ent.com.**

11-11-15

"You may delay, but time will not."
~Benjamin Franklin

[handwritten inscription]

Stacia,

I hope you enjoy the book & that you share a review on GoodReads.com 🙂

May the Reason be with You!

~M

10% of all author royalties are donated to children's not-for-profit organizations, primarily
Big Brothers Big Sisters of America and Junior Achievement.

Mentor • Educate • Inspire

This book is dedicated to my
remarkable daughters, Mia and Eva,
who remind me nearly daily about the improbable
gift that is pressure.

"The entire preoccupation of the physicist is with things that contain within themselves a principle of movement and rest. And to seek for this is to seek for the second kind of principle, that from which comes the beginning of the change." (Metaphysics)

~Aristotle, 340 B.C.

"The first rule is to keep an untroubled spirit. The second is to look things in the face and know them for what they are."

~Marcus Aurelius, 169 A.D.

"Fear is the path to the dark side. Fear leads to anger. Anger leads to hate. Hate leads to suffering."
~**Yoda** (A long, long time ago in a galaxy far, far away)

Whether it's a project at work or a gold medal championship performance, there's an unavoidable, integral and underlying force always at play: *Pressure*.

When you are able to fully understand and appreciate pressure for its true nature (a supernatural phenomenon), you will more naturally *accept* rather than fight, *adopt* rather than reject, and *embrace* rather than flee.

Your achievements will multiply, your contributions will become more significant, and your influence will expand far beyond your imagination.

Welcome to the Pressure Paradox.

CONTENTS

CONTENTS

FOREWORD

By David Allen

Before I share some introductory thoughts about *The Pressure Paradox*, I'd like to offer up a little background about the author that will likely add some philosophical context to what you're about to read.

Join me in a memory. We're in the living room of a weathered beach house just off the boardwalk in Pacific Beach, San Diego. It's the late '80s and Ronald Reagan is in the White House. The room is decorated in a cluttered surfboard and thrift store furniture motif, but outside the front door there's nothing but sunshine, surf and possibility. My buddy Martin Grunburg lives in the beach house every 20-year-old surfer wants to live in – a pauper's shack on a million-dollar piece of oceanfront. Above the living room window that frames the surf and sand just steps away is a torn-out advertisement from a surf magazine that reads, "Maybe the living room isn't much, but check out the front yard."

I'm reaching back for this memory because of a small detail that has stuck in my mind after all these years. Amid the clutter of *Surfer* magazines stacked on Martin's coffee table was a worn copy of the *Tao Te Ching*, an ancient classic of Chinese philosophy that can be roughly translated to *The Virtuous Way*. I remember thinking at the time that the juxtaposition of magazines celebrating the culture of surf with a classic work of Chinese philosophy was very "Martin." Even as a young man, it was in his character to be attracted to the elements – the ocean, its endless rhythms, its equilibrium, and perhaps the many truths buried amid its mysterious depths.

Martin and I have very different tastes in reading. As an English teacher, my leanings have always been toward great works of fiction that deal with universal themes and the nature of the human condition. Martin is wired differently. Anyone who has ever met him will agree that the adjectives "intense" and "engaged" apply in spades. So it's no surprise that Martin has always been drawn to literary sources of inspiration, motivation and achievement. My literary heroes are Shakespeare, Hemingway and DeLillo. Martin's literary reference points run more toward Tony Robbins, Wayne Dyer, Deepak Chopra, Norman Vincent Peal and Brian Tracy, to name a few.

In my experience, a great friend with different tastes in reading but a shared appreciation of good bourbon makes for the very best in interesting discussions. So when Martin asked me to give him notes back in 2009 on early drafts of his book, *The Habit Factor*, I was honored and very interested to see what he had going. I knew Martin had been tracking his behaviors to form good habits as he trained for endurance events like the Catalina Classic paddleboard race and Ironman competitions. As I said, we're talking about a passionate and motivated guy.

I know that most of the books that populate the "self-help" or "personal development" categories target specific topics. Be a Great Leader. Plan for a Secure Financial Future. Lose Weight. Stay Fit. So I hope I can be forgiven for expecting something along the lines of "How to Break

Bad Habits" or perhaps "How to Develop Good Habits." But as I worked my way through the draft for *The Habit Factor*, I was stunned. Within its pages I found a much deeper exploration of Habit as an elemental force that underscores *all* of human achievement. The Habit Factor delved far past any specific agendas or goals, to the most basic level of what powers successful people regardless of their fields or accomplishments.

So his objective wasn't necessarily about how some people might excel in any specific particular pursuit; rather it was an exploratory and experiential analysis of how the natural animal (human) operates within the principles of this natural world. The point I think he makes convincingly is that, once any one of us understands and then harnesses the force of Habit, we immediately become more effective and efficient, and our goals are achieved far more quickly.

So, *The Pressure Paradox*. Of course I agreed to have a look – couldn't wait, to tell the truth. But what do you think I was asking myself? Is this going to be a book about dealing with stress, or has Martin once again managed to explore new directions and places below the surface – subterranean spaces that might offer ways for us to approach Pressure differently, perhaps in the same manner he exposed Habit?

I'm happy to report that, if you've picked up *The Pressure Paradox*, you're in for a treat. In a way, *The Pressure Paradox* is the perfect companion piece to *The Habit Factor*. In *The Habit Factor*, Martin disabuses us of the fallacy that habits are "bad habits" that need to be broken. He reveals, among other things, the value of positive habit formation, how to construct supportive habits, and how critical it is to align these habits to your most important goals.

In *The Pressure Paradox*, he exposes a parallel fiction with regard to our common perception of pressure as a destructive force that works only to set us back, defeat our productivity and create distress in our lives. In the pages that follow, Martin shares how pressure is a related trait of energy that not only affects us all, but when we are able to use its force positively, we can accelerate our achievements.

I'm back in the beach house, surprised, and yet not surprised. Martin has again endeavored to bridge the gap between the organic, immediate reality of the natural world and some of man's most significant questions about how to become a better person (be more and achieve more). It's all elemental, after all. It must be; the principles will never change.

So turn the page and get ready to consider the fact that your old enemy Pressure might actually be one of the greatest secrets and ingredients to a life well lived.

Enjoy.

PREFACE

Welcome! You may be meeting this work prior to reading *The Habit Factor*, and while this is meant as a complementary volume, reading *The Habit Factor* is by no means a prerequisite.

After marinating on the captivating subject of pressure for well over four years, pressure's similarities to habit (as explored in *The Habit Factor*) are undeniable.

First and foremost, each represents a unique attribute of *energy*.

Energy accounts for *all* of life within the universe, and therefore it must be *the* essential element required for anyone to achieve any goal. In fact, the Latin root of energy is "energia" from the Greek "energos," which equates to "in work." Even physics has defined energy in the following terms: "The capacity of a body or system to do work."

Energy is the fundamental building block essential to all of our productivity and achievements, past, present and future. Therefore, the understanding, application and mastery of energy – and in particular the traits <u>habit</u> and <u>pressure</u> – are essential to optimizing your productivity, performance, and even peace of mind.

Paradoxically, contained within each of these unique attributes (timeless principles and forces) is the equal capacity to ruin your life if misapplied or misunderstood, which may explain why both habit and pressure carry a *predominately negative* association (another great similarity between the two).

Within these two books, *The Habit Factor* and *The Pressure Paradox*, any reader will find a dynamic philosophy laced with simple strategies and tactics on how best to multiply their productivity and achieve their most important goals.

As the late, great Dr. Stephen Covey used to say, "We are not in control, *principles* are in control." Indeed, principles govern our lives. Principles are timeless truths and forces that dictate particular "laws" or constraints in which, for optimal effectiveness, we must operate our lives. The beauty is, by *acknowledging* these truths we regain control by harmonizing with these natural forces.

May the pressure be *with* you.

PROLOGUE

DAVE

> *"Everyone knows they are going to die,*
> *but nobody believes it."*
> ~Mitch Albom, Tuesdays with Morrie

When you get right down to it, everything *begins* with an endpoint, a deadline. Your beginning/my beginning both contain an ending as mysterious as its corresponding origin. In fact, you might even regard this as our ultimate "deadline." This is an important consideration as we explore our personal productivity – what compels, inspires, motivates and ultimately influences a lifetime of achievements

The question really isn't *if* we might expire but *when*, and given that the *when* is a complete unknown, you'd think there might be a little bit more incentive (dare I say, *pressure*) to help us make the best use of the precious time we have.

As I was leaving my good friend Dave's place (note the Foreword), we'd just shared more than we should have of his gifted double-rye whiskey, and he said something that reverberated in my head for weeks to come.

First, let me share that Dave is brilliant! He's an academic, a great thinker (a bit of a logician), and I sense he enjoys our philosophical discussions almost as much as I do. (On occasion these discussions seem to get a little more interesting after some of his sippin' whiskey.)

There may be nobody better to bounce my ideas off. Dave was an instrumental resource as The Habit Factor approached publication. Still, I had no idea how he and one of our latest discussions might help to spark my next work – *this* work. In fact, at the time I really had no idea there even *was* a "next" book.

As I rode my bicycle home, I kept thinking about what Dave said as I walked out the door.

"You've always been great at that."

"What?" I asked, holding the door and looking back.

"Your ability to commit – to stick to a deadline."

It's a bit ironic now as I write this because as I recall we were discussing *his* book – the one that had been in the works for months and now, as it turns out, years.

Then it hit me.

Regardless of any past achievement, I didn't have to look too far to find a sort of culminating episode – often a deadline, sometimes a performance date, such as a triathlon, or even self-imposed deadlines as with writing a book, developing apps, starting companies, introducing products or services, etc.

Wait, I can hear you now: "Having a deadline to enhance productivity or accelerate creativity is hardly a new revelation." Correct! In fact, it's often a requirement – a critical component in any productivity puzzle and one that should not go without notice.

However, if we look a little deeper something far more mysterious and significant emerges, something that goes far beyond each and every deadline.

In fact, behind, within and around every deadline is a force much greater than the deadline itself – a supernatural force responsible for nearly every great invention, idea and achievement throughout history.

This force has propelled many of the greatest achievers to perform at their highest level. And, paradoxically, it's a force most often responsible for demoralizing, destroying and even debilitating those who may not have had a proper awareness or understanding of its true nature.

The **force** is *pressure – an omnipotent energy that permeates our lives. Pressure has been with us since our birth and will be with us until our last breath – and perhaps beyond.*

Interestingly, the physical laws of pressure were identified centuries ago by many of the greatest physicists and mathematicians throughout history. But what appears to have been missed is how the laws quite literally transcend the physical universe and invade the non-physical – the realm of the unseen.

Deadlines are effective because they create *pressure.* However, that statement begets some new, larger questions, such as:

What is pressure? How does it originate, or how might we apply these physical laws toward our own productivity, performance and even well-being?

Perhaps we should even ask, "Why does pressure exist?"

Recall Aristotle's quote from the beginning: "… to seek for the second kind of principle, that from which comes the beginning of the change."

"… *that from which comes the beginning of the change.*"

Fascinating.

That is what so many of us are after, isn't it?

"The beginning of the change."

I'm sure you realize a significant case can be made that the Universe itself doesn't even exist without the vital contribution of pressure.

So, if science's best guess about universal creation, the Big Bang theory, is even remotely close, then we can thank our very existence to, of all things, pressure.

A great rock-and-roll band from the '70s, The Doobie Brothers, produced a classic song called "Long Train Running (without Love)," which has the chorus, "without love, where would you be now?"

We might all very well ask the same question about pressure. Sing along, "Where would you be now – without pressure?"

It's a bit captivating to view pressure in this new light – **as an active participant in the creation of <u>all</u> existence, a giver of life and as purely a creative force responsible for you, the reader.** *Pressure may be the single greatest creative force in our universe.*

So you may be wondering, "When did we ever learn this in school?"

Who teaches this to us, or perhaps more importantly, to *our kids?*

PROLOGUE

I'm fairly sure there wasn't a "Pressure 101" class in high school that I could've attended or, at the very least, ditched.

WHY READ THIS BOOK

"The cave you fear to enter holds the
treasure that you seek."
~Joseph Campbell

Just how misunderstood is pressure as a subject, particularly when it comes to our productivity, performance and even, incredibly, peace of mind? Well, here's a quote from a recently published book, *Performing Under Pressure* (Crown Publishing, February 2015). In fact, this is more than just a quote – it appears to be the authors' main thesis:

"The bottom line –pressure is the enemy of success: It undermines performance and helps us fail." (The paragraph goes on to cite many supportive instances, such as pilots, surgeons, and air traffic controllers making errors, or professional athletes missing their usual shots while under pressure). "Pressure," the book asserts, "is more than a nemesis; it is a villain in our lives.[a]"

Wow! That's powerful language. It's understandable why the vast majority of people, and even these authors, might think this way about pressure. On the surface, pressure certainly appears to be the enemy. However, if we look deeper, we discover that pressure, much like what we

---

[a] Authors Hendrie Weisinger and J.P. Pawliw-Fry, Page 3, Introduction

discovered about habit in The Habit Factor, is *neither* good nor bad.

Pressure is an entirely *neutral* supernatural force. Taken a step further, due to its preeminence within our lives, it would hardly be fruitful to view pressure as the enemy. If pressure were truly the enemy, then we might as well all pack up and head home – it's time to surrender[b], we can't possibly win, right?

If we were to follow such a pervasive misunderstanding – that pressure is evil, a "nemesis" and a "villain," we should make every attempt to avoid it, right? And, unfortunately, doing so would not only prove frustrating and fruitless, but would greatly inhibit our creativity, productivity and, ultimately, even impair our personal growth.

Even the wealthiest of parents who want the very best for their children will go out of their way to ensure their kids experience some real-life pressures, such as chores or a summer job, with the hope that they'll reap all the associated benefits that come with challenge and hard work (discipline and responsibility come to mind). There is even a famous Japanese proverb that underscores this point: "Adversity is the foundation of virtue."

To be clear, we are not referring to negative peer pressure or bullying, but rather life-pressure, things such as work, chores and responsibility – knowing that is the type of pressure that teaches children important life lessons that

---

[b] Reviewed later; surrender can be a useful technique to better address pressure.

help forge their character and will serve them long into the future.

The idea that pressure is a villain or the enemy of success ultimately proves untenable in the real world.

Rather, if we choose to look deeper into pressure, what we find is that it demands our careful consideration, understanding and even, ultimately, our appreciation – the same type of appreciation you freely give to your greatest passions. After all, what is more important than your most pressing goals? Understanding how pressure is the fuel to help you achieve those goals is vital.

Not even a reality TV "star" avoids pressure all the time, as my daughter once asserted. In fact, some might even argue that due to appearances, contract obligations, etc., a "celebrity" may experience even greater pressures than the average citizen.

To view pressure another way, consider the simple act of problem solving. Any problem, by definition, involves an existing state (condition) and a desired end-state (ideal condition); the objective or goal is to bridge that gap. It's worth noting that the gap (itself, the delta) is what instantly generates a sense of *tension*, or to use its synonym, *pressure*.

And, since humans are naturally creative and problem-solving creatures, their ability to channel pressure to solve problems makes them unique. For instance, dolphins are fascinating, beautiful and highly intelligent creatures, but they are not creating microprocessors, writing screenplays (that we know of), or building motorboats, bridges or skyscrapers.

To be human, in essence, is to be creative. Have you solved any problems *recently*? Today perhaps?

Each time you solve a problem you can rest assured the solution *relieves pressure*. By its very nature, pressure is part of every problem and that pressure, when *channeled positively*, can direct you and your energies toward a creative solution to help you achieve your goals.

Please understand, I'm not referring to Michelangelo or Monet-type creativity either (although I could be). I'm talking about everyday-living creativity. The type of creativity you used when you slid the bucket of paint in front of the door to keep it open while you were carrying groceries in and out of your house.

As much as this book is about helping you to be less stressed, more relaxed, peaceful, balanced and even happier, this book is *more* about helping you truly understand pressure from a number of important vantage points. When you do, the common troubles and worries associated with pressure are likely to take on a slightly different light.

I'm fairly certain there isn't anyone who you or I might consider "successful" who hasn't *positively* channeled pressure to help them meet their goals and ideals.

To test this theory, let's use some quick analysis and a little reverse-engineering. Consider any historic great or personal hero, and then please ask yourself, "Did they experience any pressures in their life?"

For instance, let's examine former president Abraham Lincoln. Did Abraham Lincoln become a legendary president (perhaps the greatest of all time) *in spite of* the pressures in his life (wife died young, defeated in numerous elections, bankruptcy, depression, slavery, Civil War, etc.), or were his character and greatness codified, galvanized and ultimately defined because of these repeated pressure-filled experiences?

It's worthwhile to perform this exercise for any personal hero or historical "great." Consider, for instance, Winston Churchill, Martin Luther King, Helen Keller, Gandhi or Mandela, just to keep this list very short

You can probably guess how the exercise ends: Each, without exception, endured enormous pressures that ultimately proved to be both foundational and instrumental to their success.

How about we scrutinize another modern American hero, the late, great Steven Jobs (founder of Apple)?

It's widely known that Steve Jobs faced enormous pressures, particularly when he regained control of Apple in 1998. The company was a fast-sinking ship and near bankruptcy.

One of his first objectives was to gain access to badly needed capital. In order to do this, Jobs settled a long-standing and costly lawsuit with Microsoft and at the same time creatively bargained to have Microsoft extend its support and development of the Microsoft Office suite for the Macintosh platform.

Later, in 2003, Jobs was diagnosed with pancreatic cancer. Consider the pressure such a diagnosis must have created – yet oddly, that may have been the very catalyst to fuel Jobs' and Apple's rapid ascent and innovative surge.

Even Jobs' now-famous Stanford commencement address of 2005 seems to support this premise, particularly when he shares some insight into the mindset his disease instilled: "Remembering that I'll be dead soon is the most important tool I've ever encountered to help me make the big choices in my life."

What if Jobs and these other "heroes" we've seen throughout history recognized that their life pressures could facilitate and ultimately help to fuel their ambitions?

Taken a step further, rather than being the "enemy" of success, what if pressure were actually a personal ally? A supernatural force made readily available to any one of us, at any time, to help us combat the *real enemy*: ourselves – our doubts, fears and insecurities.

THREE CIRCLES

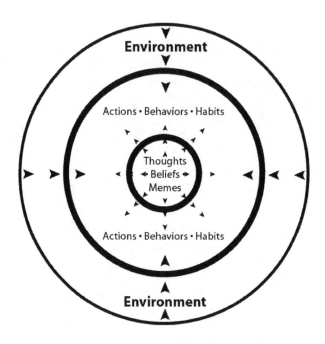

"Genius can be recognized by its
childlike simplicity."
~Chinese Proverb

Analyze this diagram above carefully and in the most simplistic terms, it represents the *entire* context of human behavior, bookended and influenced by just two "worlds": our inner, invisible world (thoughts) and our outer, physical world (environment).

Since the dawn of man, the great philosophers have promoted and taught that it is the "first world," our thoughts (the inner world), which directly influences and impacts our outer world. In fact, in the late 1800s William James proclaimed, "The greatest revolution of our generation is the discovery that human beings, by changing the inner attitudes of their minds, can change the outer aspects of their lives."

Brian Tracy simply suggests this: "High achieving men and woman are simply those who know how to use their minds better then low achieving men and women."

The essence of that statement is really in the "use of their minds," which, of course, infers better thinking.

At this point, please don't get caught up trying to understand what "better" or more accurate thinking is. The key idea for *now* is to focus on the core statement, which is that our thinking directly influences our environment, which represents the tangible results in our life – our outcomes and experiences.

While this may seem overly simplified, it cannot be overstated because, as you likely already know, more often than not thought precedes both emotion and action (that is, behavior and feeling.) For instance, if you concentrate your thoughts upon an unsatisfactory outcome – that you're going to miss a rock concert or playoff game that you've wanted to see your entire life – you'll *feel* disappointed.

So, how does pressure come into play?

Interestingly, pressure works its magic from both ends of this circular equation. In its physical form pressure contains, influences and directs our attention (pushing inward), and is representative within our environment. A simple example of this might be an extremely hot day (environment), which directs our attention and thoughts toward finding a way to become cooler and more comfortable: Environmental pressure is directing our thoughts and then influencing our actions.

In its invisible form, concentrated thought can manifest into pressure, thereby directing behavior. For instance, the repeated thought that "I must get this book finished" creates pressure that ultimately drives my writing behavior – which, with consistency, becomes a habit and ultimately results in a physical book. This is an example of inner-world pressures altering my outer-world actions and physical environment.

With this awareness, the key to any behavior change, including goal achievement, is to address both sides of the equation.

This becomes a simplified framework for behavior modification and can be applied to anything, whether it is to quit smoking, be more social, or to be more productive. At its essence, there are only two critical factors that either aid or impair your productivity efforts: your thoughts and your environment.

Therefore, to accelerate any desired outcome, to achieve any particular goal, you should thoroughly analyze your two circles or "worlds" – the inner and outer environment.

As another example, let's consider a smoker's desire to quit smoking. The first thing she probably ought to do is focus first on all the external factors within her environment. This might include throwing away her cigarettes (any inventory). This may sound rudimentary, but it immediately changes her environment to one that *inhibits* the act of smoking.

Then, moving to the inner circle, mentally she must commit to not purchasing cigarettes. To reinforce this mental framework, you might carry painful images of lung cancer victims (remember those "truth ads"?).

Additionally, she would put in writing her commitment about what it means to be cigarette-free and all the related benefits, and then sign and date a contract. Then she would have a spouse or close friend (an accountability partner) acknowledge and cosign this document. These efforts all help to shape the internal landscape and her thoughts.

Failure in behavior change most often occurs when you address only one side of the equation.

For instance, you may readily commit to not eating potato chips at night (an inner circle parameter). Yet, the very act of keeping potato chips in your pantry (environment: an outside parameter) is likely to ultimately derail your efforts.

Environment – the outside circle – will almost always defeat your inner commitment because willpower tends to wane with personal energy reserves.[1] This is why, for instance, one of the great Alcoholics Anonymous sayings is, "If you don't want to slip, stay away from slippery places."

This is also the same sort of understanding that sparked an entire company known as KitchenSafe (featured on Shark Tank, a TV show where successful investors listen to entrepreneurs' pitches and, on occasion, offer to invest in new startups). The founders of KitchenSafe[c] created a time-locking container designed to help you curb your desires (and behaviors) by helping you to lock up whatever your craving might be.

Are you tired of seeing the kids play with their phones during dinner? Then lock them up until after dinner. Maybe you want to lock up all your cookies until you drink eight glasses of water for the day – lock them up! Whatever the desired behavior, KitchenSafe helps to modify the environment (adding an impediment), which then helps to reinforce good behaviors.

When it comes to eliminating your bad habits, a quick tip is to remember the three "Ments."

Environ*ment*! (add steps, use impediments!)

Replace*ment*

Experi*ment*!

First, be sure to assess and then alter the environment to ensure it supports your desired outcome. It's important to understand how much environmental pressures dictate our behavior. Consider how you might behave in a hospital or in a church versus a bar or nightclub.

So, in order to tailor your behavior you first want to modify your environment, and the easiest way is to begin by removing anything that supports your bad behaviors (again, chips in the pantry, cigarettes in the car). Understanding where and what the environmental cues are that trigger the

---

[c] http://www.thekitchensafe.com

bad habit will help you to develop a new, supportive environment that helps to cultivate the new, positive habit[d].

Next, it's important to remember that nature (which abhors a vacuum) and science urge us to *replace* any bad habit with a good one. Eliminating a bad habit is much easier when you are replacing it with a supportive, positive habit. The Dutch theologian Desiderius Erasmus wisely noted, "A nail is driven out by another nail. Habit is overcome by habit."

Finally, it's essential to test new variations with new behaviors, to experiment and be patient. *The Habit Factor* was born from these kinds of behavior experiments. And now, in many ways, *The Pressure Paradox* expands upon these experiments.

A quick (but not easy) experiment you might consider is to switch up some of your affiliations and social circles, perhaps even friendships, since our social circles exert enormous pressure (for better or worse) upon our behavior. A simplified example of this you've probably already noticed is that smokers will hang out with other smokers, yoga people will be in the company of other yoga people, cyclists befriend other cyclists, etc.

You've probably heard the old adage, "Birds of a feather flock together." A favorite and related quote I like is from former football head coach Bill Parcells, who once quipped, "Creatures of similar plumages habitually congregate in places of closest proximity."

---

[d] Assuming you use P.A.R.R. methodology and you are tracking!

Funny.

In a fairly recent interview by Lifehacker.com, author Tim Ferriss offered the following as the *best advice* he'd ever received:

"You are the average of the five people you associate with the most."

Tim is best known for his ability to hack away at the non-essential many to get to the core few to amplify one's results. So, when he suggests that is the most significant advice he's ever received, it's worth giving it a second look.

How affirming is that statement about *your* immediate social environment? I'm not sure if he means the average of everything across the board, IQ, EQ, finances, net worth, etc., but it does not necessarily matter; the key is his (and hopefully your) enhanced awareness that your immediate social environment contributes *significantly* to your overall achievements. And why wouldn't it? Based upon the diagram at the beginning of this section, your friends are, in essence, rotating around you in the outer circle and your closest friends have the closest proximity.

Do you not think they influence your behavior? Does their influence not correspond to your productivity and performance?

So, back to Coach Parcells, a man who knows a thing or two about success and winning after two Super Bowl championships as well as encountering many (difficult, losing) seasons over his 19-year career as a head coach. He was very familiar with the sort of distractions that might interfere with his team's championship aspirations. He understood that all it would take is one or two "bad apples" in the locker room disrupting the entire team's chemistry.

When it comes to our social circle, or even our professional teams, we can learn a lot from these observations.

What does your social and championship team look like? These could include your friends, partners, associates, professional counsel, etc. How are you building, enhancing, recruiting, modifying and pruning those influences?

After all, it's the related pressure of the associated social environments that drives these behavior norms, expectations and even laws!

Twenty years ago there were very few kids wearing helmets on bicycles. Today, if your 11-year-old rides a bike just one block without a helmet, you're considered an irresponsible parent.

Further, it's practically unheard of for any 11-year-old (in our social circle) *not* to have a cell phone. I know that sounds a bit crazy, but it's true. Does that make it right? Certainly not, but the point is this is representative of our environment – and it's our environment that drives and shapes our expectations and corresponding behavior. If you've ever heard the saying "keeping up with the Joneses," you know this to be true.

What about kids who grow up in impoverished and crime-ridden neighborhoods? Unfortunately, all the education, training and persuasion in the world will have only a limited influence compared to their immediate environmental surroundings.

The environment *doesn't always* win, as I noticed a popular author tweeted the other day. However, it *almost* always wins.

Mayor Giuliani of New York (January, 1994-December 31, 2001) applied the influence of environmental pressure to modify behavior when, in his second term, he hired Police Commissioner William Branton, who was an ardent proponent of the "broken window theory"[2] of law enforcement.

A driving idea behind the "broken window theory" is that of "zero tolerance" for petty crimes and the immediate repair/removal of vandalism (broken windows, graffiti, etc.). While the philosophy and program had its detractors, the results were unmistakable. Crime was down, citizen confidence and optimism were up – the environment just "felt safer," as one New Yorker put it.

In this light, the success of the program becomes much easier to understand. When your environment improves, *expectations change* and the correlating behaviors adjust – just another example of how our environment (whether it's tailored intentionally or not to support our goals) will influence and guide our behaviors, thoughts and ultimately our results.

Introduction

Jerry: No offense, but I don't believe the Red Sea story and I don't believe in "six days to create the world."

GOD: You're right.

Jerry: I am?

GOD: Tell ya the honest truth, I thought about it for five days and did the whole job in one. I'm really best under pressure.

Oh, God! 1977
George Burns as God
John Denver as Jerry

PRESSURE IN A DIFFERENT LIGHT

"If you want to find the secrets of the universe, think in terms of energy, frequency and vibration."
~ Nikola Tesla

While attempting to peel a banana on a local street corner, a tourist noticed a bunch of local children laughing at his efforts.

"Why are they laughing at me?" he wondered.

It turns out the man peeling the banana was going about the process as most of us tend to do, beginning at the top end of the banana, the stem, and peeling toward the bottom.

The man was astonished to learn that this process is precisely the opposite of how the locals peeled their bananas.

One of the boys demonstrated, showing him that it was the bottom of the banana that was the most ripe; it would open easily simply by pinching it. The result was stress-free banana peeling toward the stem.

I've shared this story now dozens of times in recent years, either in a workshop or when I witness someone struggling to peel their own banana. What makes this simple adjustment so remarkable is that it shifts a recurring behavior (habit) that is repeated by the vast majority of people (peeling a banana incorrectly, or at the very least inefficiently), and it literally flips or inverts the process and behavior 180 degrees, giving us a radically different way to view a previously familiar act.

Chances are fairly good that what we have learned about the subject of pressure is not unlike the act of peeling a banana. We are likely due for a 180-degree shift in our awareness and understanding.

If you read The Habit Factor, you know this is essentially the same realization we came to regarding habit. Incredibly, both habit and pressure carry a predominately negative set of connotations (at least within Western society).

Rather than learning about either of these subjects in any direct fashion (school, for instance), we have been largely subject to varied opinions, indirect lessons, and in many cases uneducated ideas about what pressure is, if it's even considered at all.

Even our direct experiences with pressure are largely tainted by societal norms and the associations we've gleaned throughout our lifetime. So, here's the scary part: What if our perception of pressure has been wrong, or maybe in the *best* case, misguided?

Do yourself a favor and pay attention to the news or perhaps just TV in general over the course of the next few days, and ask yourself what associations you identify with the word and subject of "pressure."

Far more often than not it appears that the inferred conclusion we're expected to make is: *Pressure is bad.*

However, what we continue to notice if we care to look a little more deeply is that pressure – or more importantly, how we *respond* to it – has a radical and direct influence over our ability not just to create the life we desire, but to become a healthy, productive member within our society.

This bears repeating: **How we *respond* to pressure directly correlates to our performance, overall happiness, well-being, and ultimately even our success.**

So, what did you learn about pressure in high school?

From what I can recall, there was constant pressure to prepare for and take tests. Pressure to deliver reports on time. Pressure anytime there might be a pop quiz. Pressure to present in front of your peers.

There was a constant pressure to perform – whether you were on a sports team or any team. There was even pressure always to be punctual. Pressure to have good attendance. Pressure to achieve good grades. Not to mention the pressure to qualify for and be admitted to a good college.

Perhaps most of all, there was always a constant pressure to fit in socially with our peers.

Tragically, according to the CDC, teen suicide is on the rise and accounts for an alarming 13 percent of deaths among youth and young adults aged 10-24 (much of it driven by the negative pressures of social media, cyberbullying and related stresses.)[3]

If you graduated high school and then went on to college, you recall that *pressure* was with you every step of the way – and it only intensified the closer you moved toward graduation.

Post-college you may have opted for additional education, or else you entered the "real world," determined to develop a career (further escalating the pressures). Only now, instead of competing for an A grade you may be competing to feed yourself and your family.

It all begins to sound a bit *stressful*,[e] doesn't it?

You may be wondering, "How does stress differ from pressure?" Stress, a variant of pressure, can be very detrimental in large doses. However, recent studies show that in many cases there is great value to short-term, temporary stress.[4]

But first, here's another thought to contemplate about our educational norms and pressure: What if the underlying, unintentional (and perhaps even unknown) benefit of all this education, or to be more accurate, "schooling" – the testing, the quizzes, the presentations, etc. – was that it strengthened a student's tolerance to life's forthcoming pressures?

As important as the actual subjects in school are, you could make the argument that equally important (perhaps even more important) is the ancillary benefit – the strengthening of our children to the daily pressures of school: getting up early, doing homework, studying for tests, etc. Interestingly, it is these pressures that help to galvanize character and create the habits of discipline and industry (for starters).

For many high school dropouts, the challenge isn't necessarily the difficulty of the curriculum itself. Often it's

---

[e] Soon we will delve into the important differences and distinctions between pressure and stress, two words often interchanged.

the structure: rules, class times, tests, quizzes, reports, deadlines – all the *authority*, which translates into *pressure*.

One wonders how students might respond if they were first taught to understand, recognize and better relate to pressure? What would happen if they were actually taught how pressure could be their ally and how it might serve their life's goals and achievements?

And, speaking of personal growth and education, let's try to rekindle a memory from our seventh grade science class. Do you recall any lessons about *light*?

We were all taught that light (as energy) contains various spectrums and frequencies, some of which might harm us (UV light for instance), and some that may serve us (infra-red).

Light Spectrum (Visible) (1)

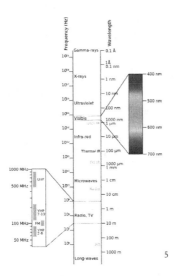

5

What might happen if people began to regard pressure in this same *light*? (No pun intended.)

Is it possible that pressure (also energy) may be similar and have both positive and negative attributes and frequencies? Better still, what if we came to recognize and understand that pressure reacts in a similar way to light as it "*refracts*" off an object?

When light refracts through a prism, for instance, it *channels* the pure white light (example above) into a visual array of distinct colors (frequencies). Note: Each color is a distinctively different frequency.

Now, consider how pressure (energy) might *refract* when it is channeled through our mind and body, or perhaps to be more accurate, our *mind-body*.

Refraction Defined

noun: **refraction**

1. The fact or phenomenon of light, radio waves, etc.,
   being <u>deflected</u> in passing obliquely through the
   interface between one medium and another or
   through a medium of varying density.
   1.1   change in direction of propagation of any
              wave as a result of its traveling at
              different speeds at different points
              along the wave front.
   measurement of the focusing characteristics

Prism: Refraction of white light for visible colors   (2)

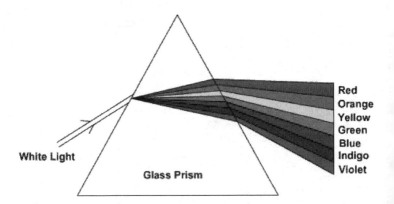

Refraction: Pencil in water and glass (3)

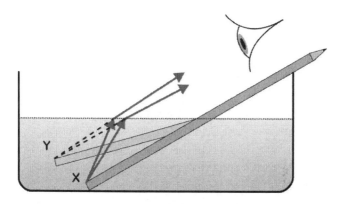

Refraction: Colors behind glass (4)

6

31

Refraction is an important concept when it comes to pressure, since we recognize pressure mostly as a <u>sensation or feeling</u>, and it's for this reason pressure has so many synonyms:

Stress
Tension
Anxiety

Looking at this Pressure Prism (illustration at the end of this chapter), we see how these negative variants come into play <u>not</u> due to the pressure itself, but as a result of our *refraction* – which is a manifestation of how the pressure we feel is interpreted and felt (*"deflected in passing obliquely through the interface between one medium and another"*).

The following definitions for each synonym (above) are important and help us to understand how each differs ever so slightly from its originating source, <u>pressure</u>.

***Stress* is felt most often when there is a disproportionate demand upon any particular resource. If a bridge is designed for a 1-ton truck and a 1.5-ton truck drives across it, the bridge is going to be stressed.**

If the college student has three tests on the same day and didn't adequately prepare or allocate her time in order to prepare, she is going to feel *stressed*.

If the kids are nagging their mom for food and at the very same time the husband is demanding her attention, the wife is likely to feel *stressed*.

The fascinating thing about stress is that biologists and psychologists have identified a positive type of stress known as eustress. Eustress is favorable, positive stress and can be characterized by short sequences or bursts of "safe" stress. For instance, playing a competitive game of cards or lifting weights are examples of eustress.

Biologists have also noted that certain healthy foods are actually stress inducing (like antioxidants), and therefore help to strengthen the immune system by stressing it ever so slightly.

***Tension* can be defined as a "degree of being stretched to stiffness." Or, a stress resulting from an elongation of an elastic body. Or, even in an artistic work, "a balance maintained between opposing forces."**

When you feel *tense* it is, in essence, the opposite of feeling loose and relaxed (remember this for later in the performance section). In fact, when it comes to peak performance, a common positive trait often cited is being loose and/or relaxed (particularly when combined with focus).

A person is likely to feel tense if she is called upon to speak, for example, or if she is about to perform, or maybe even if she is driving in traffic. Tension is often attributed to feeling ill-prepared for the activity at hand, and perhaps focusing too much on the "self" vs. the activity, performance, or even the possible negative outcomes of any particular event. As in, "I'm so tense, I know I'm going to blow it."

Anxiety is "fear or nervousness that something might happen" (Miriam Webster.com). This is characterized by a future-oriented focus (and state of being). It's a clear signal that one is removed from the moment and is anticipatory (negatively).

Lao Tzu, the great Chinese philosopher who lived approximately in the year 500 B.C., reportedly once commented, "If you are depressed, you are living in the past. If you are anxious, you are living in the future. If you are happy, you are living in the moment."

The important point here is to be mindful of the present; it is far more difficult to be anxious and/or depressed if you are completely present and in the moment. (Note: This is not meant to refer to clinical depression; rather, it's that common feeling we experience when we look negatively at ourselves or our achievements in hindsight.)

If you are anxious, your present concentration is compromised and you are future-focused.

Since living devoid of pressure is impossible, the best anyone can hope to do is *understand* it and, as Marcus Aurelius put it, **"look things in the face and know them for what they are."**

When we do this, we recognize – much like light refracting off a glass of water, distorting the image that is perceived – pressure too is "refracting" through us.

Interestingly, in the large majority of instances throughout our lives, we have the unique ability to take conscious control and positively direct the pressure we encounter.

It's important to note that it is the *refraction* (positively guided, unguided or even misguided) that directs our responses (thoughts and behaviors) and ultimately our results – *not the pressure itself.*

This is somewhat analogous to when light refracts through water in a glass (see pencil in glass, Diagram 3). The direction (positive or negative) of our refraction (energy) changes not only our thoughts, but even what we see.

That's worth repeating: How we direct pressure significantly influences where we put our attention, and therefore has the ability to alter what we actually observe!

As an example, note in Diagram 3 that the pencil is actually (physically) in one position, "X." However, based upon the refraction of light through the water, "our reality" shows the pencil in position "Y" – and that is what we actually observe. *Our perception is based upon the refraction* of the image and not the image itself.

When we apply this same principle of refraction to our own perceptions of, and reactions to, pressure, the results may look something like this: On one end of the spectrum, under extreme pressure (directed by fear and/or a feeling of prolonged hopelessness), a person may feel so overwhelmed and despondent that they may actually become suicidal.

On the other end of this spectrum (guided by purpose, hope and perhaps even faith), also under extreme pressure, an Olympian is spurred on to set a new world record. By the way, it's probably worth noting that nearly every sport establishes a new World and/or Olympic record at each Olympic Games. Care to guess the reason?

Afterward, the Olympian, a bit mystified by her stunning performance and asked to explain it, may simply say, "I guess I was just in the zone."

How is it that these two extreme pressure-filled episodes play out so differently?

How can this force be so fundamentally productive, constructive and even life-affirming, yet simultaneously (within a different circumstance) be debilitating, destructive and even invite destruction and ruin?

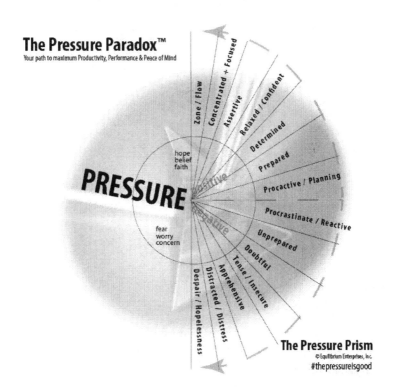

The Pressure Paradox™
Your path to maximum Productivity, Performance & Peace of Mind

PRESSURE

hope
belief
faith

fear
worry
concern

Zone / Flow
Concentrated + Focused
Assertive
Relaxed / Confident
Determined
Prepared
Procactive / Planning
Procrastinate / Reactive
Unprepared
Doubtful
Tense / Insecure
Apprehensive
Distracted / Distress
Despair / Hopelessness

positive
negative

The Pressure Prism
© Equilibrium Enterprises, Inc.
#thepressureisgood

COMFORT KILLS

"Comfort is the great enemy of success."
~Brian Tracy

It's no secret that we are living during the wealthiest time in human history. We have more creature *comforts* (interesting phrase) than any person from past generations might ever have imagined.

Sometimes I laugh when I think of what an American great like Thomas Jefferson, Washington or Lincoln might say if he saw today's common amenities, such as a smartphone, TV, or better yet, MTV!

If you are reading or listening to this book, chances are good it's on an electronic device (Kindle, iPad, mobile phone, etc., or you may even be listening to it on audio in your car either stuck in traffic or as you're whizzing along at 65 mph). This all suggests you most likely live in a fairly modernized society – a society where great value is placed upon services and products that provide comfort.

You are likely the type of person who may be looking for an "edge," perhaps a tip, tool, technique or even a device or mindset that will help you to be even more productive and/or help you achieve your goals more quickly.

Given this assumption, ask yourself this simple question: *On a scale of 1-10, how comfortable am I*? (10 representing the most comfortable you could be).

So, how comfortable are you?

When answering, you should contemplate your basic needs: food, clothing and shelter. I, for instance, could safely say I'm an 8 or a 9. (I would probably answer an 8.5, but realistically a 10 might be more accurate. Still, I always like to think there is room for improvement.)

Before I get to the follow-up question, I want you to think about your current, most important goal. You know, the one you swore on January 1st would happen *this* year. It might be getting out of debt or finishing that book or screenplay you've had shelved for the last five years. Maybe it's that trip to Spain you've talked about for the last eight years, etc.

So, here's the follow-up question:

"If I don't take action today/now, what will the consequences be?" (Again, please use a scale of 1-10, 10 being the worst.)

Chances are fairly good that the "real" consequences fall somewhere between 1 and 3, meaning you can always put it off until *tomorrow*.

If you don't deal with that debt today, chances are it will still be there tomorrow (our government knows a thing or two about this). If you don't start writing that book today, chances are good you'll still eat your lunch later. If you don't make that phone call to the travel agent about that family trip to Spain, you'll still have a place to sleep tonight.

Admit it: As things stand for you, at this immediate moment, the consequences for you *not* taking action now/today for the most part are either *low* or *extremely low*.

If that is NOT the case 1) you probably wouldn't be reading this and, 2) since you are reading this, you might congratulate yourself since it appears you have a very real sense of urgency and you will be able to put it to good use!

For the large majority, a sense of urgency tied to any particular big goal is nearly nonexistent. You *might* take action today, or tomorrow, or next week, or in a few months, and the consequences will be …?

"Without a sense of urgency, desire loses its value," Jim Rohn was fond of saying.

I once heard John Assaraf (successful entrepreneur, author, speaker and contributor to the ever-popular *The Secret*) put it this way: "Chances are good that you are probably only *interested* in your goals," but, he goes on, "the question really is, are you *committed*?"

You are no doubt interested in losing weight, but are you committed?

You are probably interested in getting out of debt, but are you committed?

The thought of doubling your company's sales is certainly interesting, but are you committed to the prospect?

Intuitively I think we all understand the difference: The committed person will do whatever it takes (hopefully within reason and the bounds of their values and morals), while the interested person has limited "skin-in the-game."

My partner once shared with me a funny story about how at a company he worked for many years ago, nothing made his sales manager happier than seeing one of the new salespeople on the team roll up in a brand-new, expensive car. Why? Well, the manager knew that meant the sales guy was going to be *on his toes*, hustling to ensure he'd make new sales – committed to keeping his fancy ride and making those car payments.

People who are just "interested" register about a 3 percent on the *change/pressure meter* – that is, they are devoid of any pressure, which of course yields zero change.

There's an old business fable about a pig and a chicken who decide to open a restaurant. As they deliberate about the name of the restaurant, the chicken proposes "Ham & Eggs." The pig objects and says, "No thanks...you'd only be 'involved,' but I would be fully committed!"[7]

More often than not, committed people channel pressure to help them overcome challenge. "Committed" people intentionally and sometimes even unintentionally use the pressure to solve their problems, to create a difference to achieve their goals.

So, back to *you*. Who is responsible for creating pressure – a sense of urgency – in your life? Who is going to take you from the realm of "interested" (no pressure) to "committed" (pressure)?
(We will review various techniques in the Application section later about how to constructively apply the pressure!)

With a limited sense of urgency, those "tomorrows" very quickly turn into "somedays," such as, "Someday I'll visit Sweden," as a 70-year-old lady told me the other day.

All I could think was (sadly), "Lady, if you haven't done it yet, chances are pretty good it isn't going to happen." Not because she's 70 but because it was clearly an interest, "someday" and not a commitment.

Anytime someone says that extra-soft and fluffy keyword "someday," it's almost always an "out" – it's an "interest" (*maybe*), but hardly a commitment.

"Someday" provides no deadline, contains zero specificity, and ultimately equates to zero pressure. As I once overheard a consultant say, "Soft people like to use soft language."

Ouch.

When it comes to productivity, the math is simple: Limited pressure equals limited or no action.

To the uninitiated, "someday" has turned into the eighth day of the week, you know: Monday, Tuesday, Wednesday, Thursday, Friday, Saturday, Sunday, *Someday*.

You and I (as products of today's Westernized society) are far more comfortable than we'd like to admit (which, ironically, would make that an uncomfortable insight).

Brian Tracy shares this little gem:

"Comfort is the great enemy of success."

Please allow that statement to sink in.

Mr. Tracy is *not* saying that comfort is the enemy of success. Rather, he's saying it's the *great* enemy of success! Talk about specificity!

One of the chief fundamental hurdles for people in the pursuit of greatness, or perhaps even just daily productivity, is our biological predisposition for comfort. Simply put, we are all wired to seek comfort (which is a form of security).

Thus, we are constantly at odds with our own self, torn between two great polar forces representing competing interests. On one side is the desire to achieve more, to excel, to be "someone." On the other is an innate desire for constant security and greater levels of comfort.

In Maslowian terms, once our basic human needs are met – food, water, clothing and shelter – our minds and (perhaps even at a biological level) our cells surreptitiously shift. We're reminded, almost relentlessly, about how comfort may be only a few feet away, be it a fluffy couch, a big bag of potato chips, or perhaps, a nice, cold beer – who knows, maybe ESPN is on TV?

While a Neanderthal's sole focus was on making it through the day alive, our senses are giving us the green light, all systems go! Prepare for comfortable times ahead!

It sounds almost comical. Yet, this is a very real and daily constant struggle for many people. For the most part, we live in an extremely "comfortable" environment. If you happen to be a citizen of a First- or even Second-World country, chances are you know this to be true.

In contrast, you can be assured George Washington wasn't kickin' it on his couch watching ESPN, downing a cold one with his buddies, or out shopping at the mall with his girlfriends.

Each of these interests – our desire for producing more, to be *somebody*, and our biological desire for increased comfort – are constantly at odds, competing for our attention

So, how can we *effectively* address this? How does anyone really deal with this conundrum?

Herein lies one of the great paradoxes of the human condition, and in many regards it is a big "Why" behind this work.

THE DRIFTER

"Drifting is a habit taken on by the
law of cosmic habit force ... "
~Napoleon Hill

If you have ever known or met a "drifter" (and chances are good you have), you recognize that more often than not, this a person with good intentions, but who appears to have been left behind, possibly scarred by a challenging upbringing or failed efforts and ventures in the past. The drifter appears to generally lack motivation, direction and/or purpose, hence the "drifter" moniker.

The drifter tends to turn a "failed" *event* into a personal label, as in, "I am a failure," which unwittingly begins to define her own self-worth and character.

Unfortunately, while carrying around such a self-defeating label, the drifter has a hard time self-correcting. Over time, drifting becomes second nature (a habit). Ultimately, setting any course of action begins to feel unnatural since it challenges their self-image and creates pressure. Drifting, as we know it, for the most part remains a *pressure-free* endeavor.

Napoleon Hill, author of *Think & Grow Rich*, an all-time bestselling self-help book originally released in the late 1930s, suggests that in many cases a drifter might be identified by the following negative traits (which, by the way, require little to no self-control): enjoys judging people, talks behind others' backs and likes to point fingers. The drifter will habitually complain and is typically very quick to tell you all the faults of his boss, friends, family, company and/or country and government. He may even insist that he has "answers." However, when it comes to real action, there are only excuses reinforced with more talk.

A drifter typically lacks emotional control, tends to be intolerant of others, and all too often is sick or ailing from real – or in many cases imagined – causes.

A telltale sign of the drifter is one of limited interpersonal skills (largely incompatible with others and has very few long-term relationships). Finally, the drifter rarely if ever considers self-improvement, as it is an entirely foreign concept. To the drifter, it is a "the world needs to improve, not me" mentality.

As Napoleon Hill correctly points out, drifting becomes a habit and needs to be addressed quickly, or eventually a perpetual drifter regresses further into greater and greater inactivity, which ultimately turns into hopelessness.

James Allen, in his classic book *As a Man Thinketh*, described drifting this way: "Until thought is linked with purpose there is no intelligent accomplishment. With the majority the barque of thought is allowed to drift upon the ocean of life. Aimlessness is a vice, and such drifting must not continue for him who would steer clear of catastrophe and destruction."

Pretty strong stuff.

"Laziness," French author Jules Renard once affirmed, "is nothing other than the habit of resting before you are tired."

The good news is drifters are made, not born, and therefore they can be unmade. In nearly all cases drifters have not been coached or mentored – encouraged to keep moving toward their ideal future, taking baby steps, developing supportive, positive habits.

Unfortunately, the drifter begins to believe that the safest course of action *is* the safest course of action, often interpreted as non-action or perhaps even worse, a consistent pursuit of pleasure.

Such a person might be analogous to a small sailboat sent out to sea with no particular destination or aim, no direction, no guiding point – truly a pleasure cruise. In the best-case scenario, the drifter is just hoping to return to the starting point unscathed. Unfortunately, if she does return, she'll literally be right back where she started, only it may be a year, two or five later – precious time wasted.

Ask any "drifter" what he thinks about the idea of pressure, and if he thinks anything of it, he might tell you a tall tale about how the "man" has created all this pressure with "modern society," or how the government or big banks or corporate America is holding him/us all down.

What was "Occupy Wall Street" about? One could make the argument it was as much about dethroning a broken investment banking system as it was a common platform and device to unite so many aimless drifters.

Chances are the drifter would be quick to assure you that pressure is "man-made," or a "real bummer," a negative consequence of modern civilization. You can be fairly certain he'd never distinguish pressure as a galvanizing force able to help forge one's character, an integral tool essential to achievement. And he's unlikely to tell you that pressure is a natural phenomenon, one that's existed since the beginning of time.

Chances are good the drifter is unaware that he's taking great pains to avoid pressure, which is unfortunate, as we recognize the futility of such an endeavor. And, much like a lioness fed in captivity – where there is little challenge or adversity to keep her survival skills sharp – hunting skills diminish ever so slightly each day. She actually becomes more enslaved, not by the bars themselves, but by the comfort of captivity.

Similarly, the drifter becomes imprisoned by his own constant quest for comfort. His own survival skills, within a pressure-filled, deadline- and responsibility-driven society, slowly begin to fade. He grows weaker, not stronger; his marketability and his desire mutually subside until his ability to provide value and service fully erode, and it's all due to his inability to appreciate and understand the immense value and benefit pressure provides.

There is, of course, "healthy" drifting and it's altogether different. A healthy drifter is often a young adult trying to identify a first career path, or she might be a person who has recently accomplished something of significance or someone transitioning from one career to another.

It's easy to distinguish the healthy drifter because her self-confidence remains intact, and even without a certain sense of direction, she is interested in taking action and attempting new endeavors. Most importantly, she understands the value and real meaning of failure and setbacks. To her, failure is feedback; it is information resulting from an event in exchange for her effort, which further assists her future endeavors.

The healthy drifter is not bitter about an unjust or "corrupt" world or corporate America, but operates from a hopeful, positive paradigm where action is the order of the day. She is not mired in anger, hate and indecision.

Einstein reportedly once commented, "The single most important decision we can make is whether we believe we live in a friendly or hostile universe."

First, it's important to recognize there is ample evidence to suggest that we live in a hostile and unfriendly universe. Just watch Animal Planet for an hour or so. The point is, we could easily validate either perspective. It is important to understand that we get to make a choice: What information are we going to seek out to validate our opinion?

There is some science behind this phenomenon, and it leads us to something in our brains known as the Reticular Activating System (RAS). In a world of unlimited information, the RAS helps to prevent us from going into complete overload by filtering information. What's interesting is it's our job to tell the RAS what to seek out. We are pre-wired to seek out and identify many patterns.[f] A

---

[f] http://www.ted.com/talks/michael_shermer_the_pattern_behind_self_deception

simple example might be buying a new car and then noticing that same type of car seemingly everywhere you go, yet you never noticed it prior to purchasing the vehicle.

For an amazing example of this phenomenon, and to witness the RAS in action, I recommend you watch this video[g] hyperlinked below or do a search for "the invisible gorilla."

These examples point to the fact that it is far easier to remain positive and take constructive, supportive steps toward our goals when we believe (we've made a choice) that a better future is possible – that, in fact, the universe is friendly.

This sort of choice and belief also fosters a special character trait, a trait so vital that Aristotle once asserted it was the single virtue upon which all other virtues must rely, and therefore he termed it the "mother of all virtues."

Care to guess what the virtue is?

John Wayne once described it this way: "Courage," he said, "is being scared to death and saddling up anyway."

The belief that the universe is "friendly" helps to foster the development of courage.

It turns out that what many drifters lack is not vision or even dreams or ideals. Many drifters can tell you about big dream and big ideals, and many enjoy talking about big

---

[g]http://www.theinvisiblegorilla.com/gorilla_experiment.html
http://blog.ted.com/wheres_the_gori/

plans. However, what they really lack is the *courage* to execute the steps necessary to make these dreams a reality.

While I hope this doesn't offend anyone, the flip side is it may create some discomfort or a little *pressure* – maybe even enough to help drive some new behaviors and change.

"A goal," Bruce Lee once pointed out, "is not always meant to be reached; it often serves simply as something to aim at." The very existence of a goal generates pressure, which helps to create and direct one's energy. This is the sort of thing that excites the "go-getters" of the world, who often become addicted to this sort of energy rush. Whereas, unfortunately, the drifter just dawdles, stalls, delays – trapped in indecision. He may even become stuck in a lonely place we touched on earlier, referred to by Brian Tracy as "Someday Isle," a sad, desolate and lonely little piece of land devoid of any pressure.

"At a certain point," Tony Robbins often will say, "it's either inspiration or desperation that helps people to take action."

Watch nearly any children's TV show and there is likely one episode where the scrawny kid who has been regularly bullied finally has had enough. He's tired of all the harassment and he's not going to take it anymore. Ultimately, he even *surprises himself* by standing up to the bully.

Similarly, there comes a point in time for many drifters when the "bully" is simply the result of prolonged periods of inactivity – a manifestation of extended meaninglessness, doing so little for so long with no direction (whether driven by fear or something else). Finally, just like the little kid being bullied, the drifter snaps out of it and says, "That's it – I'm not going to take this anymore!"

What happens next is even better: The pressure that was once holding the drifter back *inverts*. Rather than working against her, pressure becomes a motivating force to propel her toward action and future change!

REVIEW: INTRODUCTION
QUESTIONS AND ACTIONS

- Do you think you know when you are going to die?
- If science's best guess about universal creation has pressure responsible as its flashpoint, how important do you think pressure will be for your own personal creativity?
- What is the common connotation (positive or negative) that pressure has in today's news and media outlets?
- How do your react to the word "pressure" – positively or negatively?
- How many BIG goals do you currently have? Which is the most *pressing*?
- What are the current deadlines and/or timelines for these goals?
- What two qualities make deadlines effective? (pressure and consequences)
- What is the second kind of principle that Aristotle sought?
- With the right attitude, can a person develop a healthy tolerance and become conditioned to pressure?
- What is the difference between hope-directed and fear-directed internal pressure?
- What are the two "worlds" that direct our behavior? From which does pressure operate?
- What should a smoker first focus on to quit smoking?
- To accelerate behavior change or goal achievement, how can you change your environment?
- How does your net worth compare with that of your five closest friends?

- How does your peer environment alter expectations about your dress, the way you raise your kids, etc.?
- Why was the broken window theory so effective?
- Is pressure contained within every problem?
- How does comfort harm goal achievement?
- When it comes to your goals, how comfortable are you?
- Are you interested or committed?
- On a scale of 1-10, what is the pressure you feel to take action today/now on your biggest goal?
- Who's responsible for creating pressure in your life?
- How would you define the human productivity conundrum?
- Do you know any drifters?
- How do drifters respond to pressure?
- What is the #1 virtue behind which all other virtues exist?
- What did Shakespeare say about "good" and "bad"?
- What two guiding perspectives influence the pressure spectrum?
- How do we biologically respond to pressure?
- What problems can you turn into fuel?
- Is there any major worry or fear that you could accept, if only mentally, to realize a sense of peace?
- Affirmations: What mindset can I take to become more open?

Be sure to visit:
ThePressureParadox.com/prism for your **FREE**
Pressure P.R.I.S.M. Assessment!

Actions!

- ⏱ Consider how pressure (energy) might *refract* when channeled through your mind and body (mind-body).
- ⏱ Pinpoint times in the past when you may have experienced pressure as stress, tension or anxiety.
- ⏱ Think of a current stressful situation you are in. Put your attention on the present; remove negative feelings.
- ⏱ Identify your comfort level on a scale of 1-10. Choose one action you can take today that will disrupt your comfort level – just a little.
- ⏱ Interest vs. commitment: Isolate one action you can take immediately to move from the realm of "interested" to committed.
- ⏱ Identify any signs of unhealthy "drifting" in your own life/character. Determine an ideal destination and move there – take action today/now.
- ⏱ Adopting a positive mindset, make a choice to *believe* that a better future is possible. Instead of thinking about why it isn't, list 10 reasons why it is!
- ⏱ Find examples of ways you could harness courage in your life, right now, to make a positive change.
- ⏱ Take inventory of the goals that are sitting on your back burner – achievements you are "interested in." Pick one to which you can _commit_.

PRODUCTIVITY & PRESSURE

"To think is easy. To act is difficult.
To act as one thinks is
the most difficult."
~ Johann Wolfgang Von Goethe

"Make no small plans, for they have
no power to stir the soul."
~Niccolo Machiavelli

DEATH OF AN ENTREPRENEUR

"However long the night, the dawn will break."
~ African proverb

November 18, 2011, I received an email with some tragic news. As part of an entrepreneur-peer organization, emails from the group are the norm; however; nothing about this email was normal. A member was notifying our chapter that he'd just lost a dear friend to suicide.

Unfortunately, unlike my immediate friend sharing the news, his close friend apparently didn't have any peer group – no one to share his burdens, trials, challenges, pain or even the successes that are woven so tightly within any entrepreneurial venture.

The entrepreneur was only 39 and must have felt isolated, alone, worried. We can only speculate that he was feeling unimaginable pressure. At perhaps the deepest level he must have believed there was nowhere to turn and, unfortunately, nobody who might be able to help him to *displace* the pressure.

As I write this now and look back, I find it even more chilling, as my friend's email actually underscores the following sentence:

"Simply a constant pressure to perform."

Here is the actual email (excerpt):

A friend of mine committed suicide yesterday. He was an entrepreneur just like all of us.

*He was not fortunate enough to have the peers that we all have. It is a lonely place out there; we all have taken on lots of responsibility. We are the change makers of this world, and with that comes a huge amount of burden and pressure. Every day our families, friends, clients, employees and vendors are observing us. **Simply a constant pressure to perform.***

EO has given us an opportunity to have an outlet, to have a place we can truly feel safe and vulnerable on all aspects of life.

...

Alex S.

This email touched us all deeply. For the next few weeks, even though I'd never met this entrepreneur, I couldn't shake this idea of pressure yet again influencing someone's outcome – in this case, the ultimate outcome. I kept reflecting upon it: the inseparable relationship of pressure and the human condition.

Recently, a friend and a great entrepreneur confided (as we were discussing this topic) that he too had an episode of immense pressure a few years back that triggered a debilitating nervous breakdown.

The short story was that his partner did some terrible things to undermine his company once they decided to split up. What made the split even harder still was that this partner controlled the finances and unfortunately, via a multitude of lies, convinced a star employee to leave my friend and go work with him.

"When I heard that," he said, "I couldn't believe it. At that moment, I truly thought I was done-for; I felt as if the world fell square on my shoulders.

"I buckled; I had to take a knee. I was there in our kitchen, just shaking. The crazy thing was, we actually had friends coming over to visit and I did my best to wave off my wife and asked her to tell them I wasn't home."

So, why share such distressing stories?

Is there anything we can learn from them as it relates to pressure-induced stress that might help us to adjust and prevent similar tragedies?

It was Shakespeare who wrote in Hamlet, "There is nothing either good or bad, but thinking makes it so." And, it was William James, often credited as the "father of modern psychology," who wrote, **"The greatest weapon against stress is our ability to choose one thought over another."**

It's astonishing how pressure via outside circumstances (in the physical realm/environment) can infiltrate our actions (behaviors) and our thoughts and how our mental "world" (inner circle) then refracts back to the physical plane. They seemingly echo back and forth endlessly – that is, until we decide to seize the opportunity, to take mindful control for how to best to direct (refract) the pressure.

DID SOMEONE SAY PASCAL?

"Il n'est pas certain que tout soit incertain."
(Translation: It is not certain that everything is uncertain.)
~ *Blaise Pascal*

Let's quickly revisit some basic physics concepts and related terms such as Force and Pressure.

First, Pressure.

Pressure=Force/Area or,

P=F/A

Now, for us to grasp more easily what that means, we should have a basic understanding of the definition of Force, since Area is relatively self-explanatory.

Force: A force is a push or pull upon an object resulting from the object's interaction with another object. Whenever there is an interaction between two objects, there is a force upon each of the objects. When the interaction ceases, the two objects no longer experience the force. Forces only exist as a result of an interaction.[h]

Force=Mass * Acceleration.

(The Second Newtonian Law)

A key takeaway, then, is that in order to experience any pressure there must be *Force*. Again, see above, "a push or pull upon an object … an interaction with an object."

---

[h] http://www.physicsclassroom.com/class/newtlaws/u2l2a.cfm

Knowing that there is no way our personal productivity can operate outside of these scientific and natural laws, a key question becomes: "What are the two objects?"

Well, as far as this relates to *your* productivity, *you* must be one of the objects, and the other must be the desired end-state or goal (which interestingly doesn't yet exist in physical form).

Looking at the formula from another vantage point: Have you ever seen a man or woman lay on a bed of nails? Have you ever wondered why their skin doesn't puncture?

This example offers us a terrific illustration of how pressure is distributed over an Area.

(Warning: Please do not try this yourself, as if that needs to be said.) If you'd like to witness this high drama for yourself, check out the link below, which is just one of the many videos on YouTube[i] showcasing the mathematical formula of pressure (which I'm sure you've memorized by now) in action!

A person lies between two boards of nails. A cinder block is placed on top of the upper board. Then an "assistant" uses a sledgehammer (yes, a sledgehammer) to hit the cinder block hard enough to shatter said cinderblock – all while a person is between the two boards with nails!

Sounds a bit crazy, I know. I suspect Mr. Pascal, the great mathematician of the 1600s, didn't have personal productivity or a bed of nails in mind as he contemplated the formula for pressure. However, he did contemplate

---

[i] https://www.youtube.com/watch?v=hG7lGZqWFpM

pressure a great deal with regard to its unique relationship to water. So, if you're more interested in seeing how that works, I invite you to search "the hydrostatic paradox" for even greater insight into the natural realm of pressure, and yes, its many paradoxical qualities!

It's probably a good idea to deviate for a moment, before we delve into the various productivity implications of this magnificent formula. Do you recall "Death of an Entrepreneur" in the previous chapter? Tragically, under extreme pressure, a great entrepreneur took his own life. We need to understand pressure better so that we might find ways to prevent such tragedies in the future. And, as it turns out, nature has once again beat science to the solution.

In fact, biologists have identified that humans under extreme stress release oxytocin (known as the "love" or "hugging hormone"), a hormone that triggers a physical craving for contact and social interaction.

Now, please reflect upon the prior formula for Pressure: $P=F/A$ – you may begin to notice an interesting phenomenon taking place.

Our biological, neurological, sociological and physiological responses to pressure appear to do all they can to implore us to increase our "Area," which would thereby reduce the pressure or stress we feel.

Think about it: How might we increase our personal Area?

Well, under the weight of such pressures, we often will find ourselves unwittingly seeking out friends, family, social groups, church groups, etc. In fact, the very term "support group" does exactly that. A support group naturally increases our personal Area, thereby diminishing the pressure we feel. After all, it's just physics at that point. Increase the Area and you diminish the pressure.

Do you think anyone is teaching that in AA meetings? They don't have to; all they know is that the support group model works.

Even at a molecular level (oxytocin), we are quite literally being urged to increase our "Area" – to go hug someone, call someone or join a support group, and so often we don't even understand why. What's interesting is that it appears science has yet to reconcile the enigma that is oxytocin and its paradoxical qualities. (See endnote, "The Two Faces of Oxytocin.")[8]

Now, let's apply this same formula toward productivity, and once again we see some terrific correlations.

The Area (A) corresponds to our resources, typically time, money and/or people. So, increasing any one of these resources expands the Area (A) of any project, objective or goal, which thereby diminishes the related Pressure (P).

For instance, if the deadline or time allocated to complete a task for a project shrinks, the Area (A) is diminished and the Pressure (P) increases.

Conversely, by increasing any of the resources – time, money and people – the Area (A) expands and the Pressure (P) subsides.

Low Pressure – distant deadline

Higher Pressure – tighter deadline

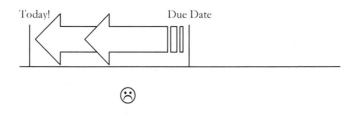

**Same tighter deadline plus increased resources
= Less Pressure**

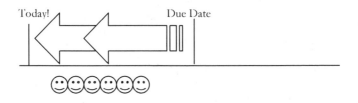

With this awareness, we have the ability to *proactively* manipulate the positive influence of pressure upon our own personal productivity, and here is the best part: *We can do this anytime we want!*

Would you like to decrease the pressure you're feeling around any particular self-directed project? The easiest way, if possible, is to extend the deadline or find a way to increase the available resources, or both.

Conversely, reducing resources or cutting the timeline will increase the pressure. What typically happens when the pressure increases? People move quicker, make decisions faster and become more creative. *Applying constraints around resources often inspires creativity and innovation.*[9]

If you're an art student and I tell you that your drawing is no longer due in two weeks, but rather is due this afternoon, and I explain that instead of using all the colors you can use only four, you are likely to immediately feel a surge of pressure.

What if I tell you that you can draw only with straight lines – that you can't use any curves?

It might be an awful drawing or it may be the most inspirational, creative and out-of-the-box drawing your teacher has ever seen.

Many writers will tell you there is nothing more terrifying than a blank sheet of paper (unlimited possibilities, no constraints and no pressure). However, wrap some constraints around what needs to be written, perhaps directed by some pointed questions that help to direct focus, and the writer will quickly have ideas about what to write.

Similarly, when it comes to speaking, if you tell a presenter that they have as much time as they need to present, the resulting presentation will be far different than if you tell them they have only five minutes. In fact, not only will the presentation be vastly different, but so will the preparation time! In many ways there is an inverse correlation between preparation time to presentation time. The less presentation time that is allowed naturally results in greater preparation time that is required.

Blaise Pascal, the great French mathematician, once wrote in a letter to a friend, "I would have written a shorter letter, but I did not have the time."

When it comes to business ingenuity, the intentional use of limitations and constraints – that is, the reduction of available resources or possible outcomes and solutions – is often at the heart of creativity, innovation and what is considered "genius."

Take Twitter, for example. Twitter is a social networking phenomenon that has grown to more than 250 million active monthly users in less than eight years. Its greatest attribute is its well-known limitation on how many characters (140) that any "tweet" (message) can contain. This was born from its early days as an SMS messaging platform that had its own constraint of 160 characters.

Then there is the iPhone. Apparently Steve Jobs, Apple's enigmatic CEO, insisted that the phone could not have more than a single "home" button. Originally, senior engineers battled Jobs, saying that it was impossible to create a phone with just a single button.

Not only was it possible, the limitation became one of the key distinctive features for a revolutionary new mobile device. Today, there is talk that perhaps Apple may even remove the "impossible" single button.

With the advent of the new Apple Watch, you can bet that the screen size will pose extreme limitations for app developers and UI designers, pressuring many of them to rethink and redesign their apps and in all likelihood make them more user-friendly.

So the next time you are low on available resources, try your best to recognize it as an opportunity to become more creative, inspired, and to be more resourceful!

Much of the advice from top entrepreneurs supports this idea. Recently, billionaire investor and entrepreneur Mark Cuban stated in an interview on Bloomberg news, "First of all, if you're starting a business and you take out a loan, you're a moron."

Here, Cuban is referring specifically to a small business loan via a bank, but really, digging deeper, the statement helps to underscore that funding anything unproven without the business first validating itself – providing sales (income) and profits – is extremely risky.

Conversely, there's something to be said for a startup business that can stand on its own, use only the resources it has and creates (being resourceful). Such a business is far more likely to succeed. As Cuban points out, many entrepreneurs think the answer to their problem lies in the funding, but that is just an excuse. Such thinking reminds me of what Dr. Stephen Covey used to say: "As long as you think the problem is *out there*, that very thought *is* the problem."

A Sense of Urgency

"I have been impressed with the urgency of doing. Knowing is not enough; we must apply. Being willing is not enough; we must do."
~Leonardo da Vinci

A well-known online consultant once put it this way in an interview: "People want to sell stuff online so they will come to me and buy our services. They know they need a website to sell. So, they'll spend the money and buy the courses and learn the skills they need. Then, they have all the tools and all the resources they need to develop a website.

"So, I'll ask them why they still haven't developed their website. And, their reply is almost always, 'I haven't had the time.'

"I then tell them, <u>Bullshit</u>! Don't F' around … don't be a F'n pussy! I think that people F around because there is no sense of urgency. So, I say, 'look I want you to imagine that Osama Bin Laden has a machine gun pointed at your family and says that you have 24 hours to collect an email address (via a website) or I'm pulling the F*ing trigger.'

"Do you think they will get that website launched?"[10]
The answer, of course, is **YES!**

While this is an extreme example with some harsh language, it quickly illustrates the depths this highly paid consultant has to go just to help rattle people out of their comfort zone – to shake them free of their daily routines and complacency.

In the National Football League there may be no better example of just how the diminishing resource of time dramatically influences a team's sense of urgency, and similarly, their productivity. Over the last 10 seasons (2004-2014), a disproportionate 27.89% of the season's total points were scored in the fourth quarter.[11] And, one wonders of those points, just how many are scored in the final two minutes?

A dramatic example was week three of the 2014 NFL season in a rematch of Super Bowl teams (Seattle Seahawks and the Denver Broncos; the latter lost in a blowout 43-8). Their 2014 game would turn out to be far more entertaining – that is, once the fourth quarter began.

Leading the game comfortably, the Seahawks were up 17-3 entering the fourth quarter. But what transpired in the fourth quarter left many a Bronco fan shaking his head. Unable to score more than just three points for the entire three quarters prior, Peyton Manning led the Denver Broncos to a remarkable 17 points in the fourth quarter. And, in the final minute of regulation, Manning drove the team 80 yards against the league's best defense to tie the game with only seconds left.

To recap: There was a total of only three points for the first three quarters and then 17 points in the fourth quarter. Unfortunately for Broncos fans, the game was then lost as the Seahawks constructed their own successful drive to win the game in overtime.

So, whose responsibility is it to modify the available resources in order to *elevate* their own sense of urgency?

Whose responsibility is it to increase a sense of urgency when it comes to achieving our own goals and ideals?

These questions remind me of an e-card found by my friend on the Internet that read:

"When is somebody going to do something about how fat I am?"

Funny. This is almost as funny:

When is someone going to apply the pressure for my goals?

Chances are good that nobody else will adjust the intensity, let's just call it "the pressure setting," for you, especially when it comes to *your own* goals, ambitions and desires.

The other day, I was working late and told my daughter I didn't want the TV on. She then asked why, and I told her I was working against a deadline for the book. She replied, "Well, it's your deadline, you can just change it." [j]

In the business world, companies rarely have a hard time applying pressure to influence their employees' behavior and improve effectiveness. A good manager

---

[j] The deadline moved at least 6 times for this book…I like to call this the *"slinky" productivity method*! BTW: Check out the physics of the slinky on Wikipedia – note oscillation and equilibrium.

seldom (if ever) ignores the power of a good deadline, quota, and any related consequences.

In fact, it's fairly common to hear something like, "Complete this project by xx deadline," or, "sell xx products in this quarter or you may be looking for a new job."

The sales profession in general is notorious for the application of *pressure* on both sides of the sales equation, the customer as well as the salesperson. Have you ever heard something like this: "Don't forget, that (widget) will be on sale only through 6 pm *tonight*."

It really wouldn't be a reach to suggest that pressure makes the *sales world* go round.

Now you may say, "Well, those sorts of tactics don't work in the long run, pressing employees all the time or pressing customers to buy." And you would be correct: Too much pressure (sustained) is often damaging, so what do we find the best managers and coaches doing? They apply the pressure and then periodically adjust and/or relieve the pressure via various techniques.

Most Fortune 500 companies offer great incentives for their salespeople – trips, rewards and recognition – all of which help to offset the pressure.

Now, let's revisit *your* most pressing goal. What (on a scale of 1-10) were the consequences if you didn't take action *today* toward your goal? Was it a 10 in urgency, or was it a 1, 2 or 3?

Here's the next question: What is the first excuse that pops into your head (honestly) when you consider your goal? How do you rationalize why you haven't taken action recently toward it?

Would taking action make you a little uncomfortable, creating any sort of pain? Are you perhaps comfortable right where you are now? Could the fear of failure be holding you back? Perhaps you fall back to the most common excuse (everyone now!): "I just don't have enough time right now."

That seems to be our (collective) best excuse, and it's no coincidence that it's also the most convenient one.

If that's the excuse, here's another question: Who has *enough* time? Who has more time?

I'm still trying to meet someone who has more than 24 hours in day. By the way, when you meet her, please tell her to give me a call.

If your excuse is not time, then the answer must be *prioritization.*

When it comes to personal productivity, I love this particular gem Brian Tracy shares, The Law of Forced Efficiency:

You'll never have enough time to do everything, but you always have enough time to do the most important things.

Very simple, very profound. In fact, the more I repeat it, the more profound it becomes.

With infinite choices to do whatever our heart desires (relatively) at any given moment, we have the ability to decide, to determine *what* to focus and concentrate upon. These decisions become the true discriminators as to whether we accomplish the things we desire in our life.

If we choose to focus (consistently) on our most pressing (interesting choice of words) goals, tasks and objectives, invariably they will get accomplished. Perhaps this is why Ralph Waldo Emerson once said, "A man is what he thinks about all day long."

However, the inability to decide, jumping from one incompatible idea or goal to the next, instantly diminishes your focus and the opportunity for accomplishment.

This bears repeating: As important (maybe more) as the work itself is the *primary act of selection*. That is, the decision about where to put your concentration becomes *the* distinguishing factor, since the work therefore must follow.

Take a moment right now and look at any object near you (audio listeners who are driving, please do not do this). Look at the object, concentrate upon it . . . now hold your attention upon it for as many seconds, hopefully minutes, as you can, as long as you can concentrate deeply upon it.

What happens? You will become aware that you are drawn to it and it seems to expand within your awareness (it even begins to consume your energy). You may even want to touch it, move it, lift it, etc.

David Allen[k], author of *Getting Things Done*, has a great saying about attention: "If you don't pay appropriate attention to what has your attention, it will take more of your attention than it deserves."

This sounds a bit like word play, but it really isn't. Those "things" that have our attention should have our awareness

---

[k] *Not to be confused with the Author of the Foreword—my buddy Dave!*

as well. Therefore, we should be conscious as to what has our attention so it isn't taking up more of our energy than it ought to. Otherwise, it's our responsibility to redirect our attention to where it needs to be.

These days, it seems everyone I know is "super busy." It becomes important "not to confuse activity with accomplishment," as the legendary coach John Wooden used to say.

Given the Law of Forced Efficiency cited above by Mr. Tracy, I've come to realize that we are not only at liberty to control those things upon which we prioritize and focus; we are *obligated* and *responsible* to consistently *adjust our comfort level, particularly regarding our most important goals.*

Mr. Tracy takes this message a bit further and introduces something he's identified as the E to E ratio: This represents your Entertainment to Education ratio, that is, the amount of time on average people spend throughout their day (and ultimately a lifetime) enjoying entertainment vs. investing in education. He believes the ratio of the average person is 50 to 1. That is, for every 50 minutes of entertainment (pressure/tension-relieving activities), there is just one minute invested toward education.

In a terrific interview with Darren Hardy, the editor of *Success Magazine*[12], Mr. Tracy comments, "You wake up, you listen to the radio, or watch the TV, then you may read the newspaper or browse the Internet. (Entertainment! Entertainment! Entertainment!) You then go to work, you chat with people, you browse the Internet (entertainment, entertainment, entertainment). Before going to bed, more Internet browsing and more TV (entertainment,

entertainment, entertainment). Then comes the weekend: movies, sports, shows (entertainment, entertainment, entertainment). It gets to the point where it's almost an obsession. People are entertaining themselves to death!"

The scary thing is that the real E to E ratio may be more like 100 to 1!

Entertainment has always been the "great escape." Nothing quite says, "I'm comfortable, I'm worry free" like kicking your feet up on the couch, flipping on the TV or heading to a movie with your friends, or any of a dozen other modern-entertainment options.

Have you seen the latest blockbuster movie? Did you go to that concert last week? How much time did you spend on Facebook or Snapchat today? You might even say to your friend, "Hey! Let's hit that party (or game) this weekend!"

Yes, we all need entertainment, clearly. That's why it's a multibillion-dollar industry. And you've surely noticed that no industry rewards its stars better. It's common to witness top athletes and actors making tens of millions of dollars each year.

By the way, what makes entertainment so splendidly valuable? Entertainment is simply getting away . . . it's that momentary escape from our daily pressures.

Do you happen to know what your E to E ratio is?

THE MOST PRODUCTIVE DAY OF THE YEAR

*"The successful man is just the
average man, focused."*
~*Anonymous*

Imagine for a minute that you have a report due tomorrow (you're almost finished), but you will have only a few hours to spend at the office before you fly out of town. BTW, you're headed to Paris for the week. Congratulations! (As long as we're going to use our imagination, we might as well have fun, right?)

There you are . . . it's the evening before your report is due and you depart at noon the next day (meaning you have to be at the airport by at least 10 am for an international flight). You figure that you'll need at least four hours of concentrated effort to complete your report, possibly six to be safe.

Your office tends to be noisy and filled with many distractions that go by names like "Jon," "Sam," "Sarah," and "Alex."

Just to keep things interesting, if your report isn't completed on time you'll likely be looking for a new job upon your return.

Here's the question: What are you going to do to get the report finished?

Chances are good you just replied, "Whatever it takes." You may even pull an all-nighter and rationalize that you can sleep on the plane. Or maybe you'll get into the office at 5 a.m. or earlier when nobody is around so you can concentrate.

Whatever your answer, you are not likely to roll into the office at 9:30 a.m. and ask Joe how his weekend fantasy football team did, or ask about the point spread for the Monday night game. You won't be chatting with Sue about how annoying Mary can be when she's always talking about her boyfriend Brad.

With your job on the line and your dream vacation only hours away, I ask you, "What sort of focus and resolve do you think you'd have to complete the report on time?"

To understand this sort of behavior (which appears to be a bit of a natural phenomenon), it may help to be introduced to a man and his "law."

The man's name is Cyril Northcote Parkinson, a British Naval historian and author who ultimately became famous for identifying this "law" (perhaps more a maxim), now widely known as Parkinson's Law. Northcote articulated rather brilliantly:

"Work *expands* so as to fill the time available for its completion."

It seems we (humans) tend to validate this "law" at almost every opportunity. The "report due tomorrow" is just a simplified example. There are really dozens of corollaries to this "law," for instance, if you have a closet, chances are you will find a way to fill it up. And if it's anything like my closet, it is overflowing. If you have a large hard drive, chances are over time you will find a way to fill that up too. The idea is that the supply of any particular resource will ultimately be met and consumed by the demands upon said resource.

Recently, the Federal Trade Commission (FTC) filed suit against AT&T claiming that users were being misled if they subscribed to the Unlimited Usage plan. Apparently, AT&T found it had to "throttle" users' bandwidth because there was only so much available spectrum, and the company underestimated the demand upon that spectrum.[13]

Time and again the demand upon a resource will be met by its availability. This is a rule more than it is a "law." It doesn't operate like gravity, but it's very helpful to be aware of. If I give you two weeks to complete a report, how long will the report most likely take you? For most of us, it's going to take exactly two weeks.

When it comes to planning events or scheduling groups of people for anything, from meetings to tee times, I've developed the habit of creating false deadlines. A noon tee time, for instance, is best preserved when I announce it as an 11:45 a.m. tee-time to the group. Not because my friends are slackers, but because of Parkinson's Law! (Well, some of them are slackers.)

For years, I've had every clock in my house and matching car clocks set seven minutes ahead of actual time, which (for a while) drove my wife a little nuts. Ultimately, though, she not only became used to it, but liked it.

If Parkinson's Law is accurate, or even mostly accurate, how can we constructively apply it to our advantage? How can we increase our output and accelerate our productivity within these seemingly natural confines of human behavior?

As long as we're at it, what prevents any of us from getting out of bed earlier, getting into the office sooner and staying at work longer?

What keeps us from working harder *and* smarter?

This is really one of the key distinctions between those we consider successful vs. the not-so-successful, and it takes us to two interesting topics.

First, the idea of being *disciplined*. "Well," you might hear someone say, "that's why Bob is such a success, because he's so disciplined . . . I'm just not as disciplined as Bob."

Garbage.

I guess that statement is only *partial* garbage, because if that is what a person believes, then they are likely to be right. As Henry Ford often shared, "Whether you think you can or you can't, you are right." Since our thoughts help to establish our boundaries and drive our behaviors, if we believe we are not disciplined, then it's hard to be wrong.

However, the "reality" is nobody is born with discipline. Have you ever met a disciplined baby? Truth is, discipline is a character trait that is crafted first via habit, which then, when established and refined over time, becomes a virtue. Hence, Bob is known to be "disciplined," but the good news is, everyone has the capacity to develop that discipline habit just like any other habit.

A man by the name of Albert E.N. Gray studied successful people and wrote a now-classic and often referenced essay, "The Common Denominator of Success." In it, Gray comes to the following conclusion: "The common denominator of success – the secret of success of every man who has ever been successful – lies in the fact that he formed the habit of doing things that failures don't like to do."

What's peculiar about this statement is Gray further observed that successful people don't like to do these behaviors either. For instance, successful people don't necessarily like to wake up early, go to the gym, eat healthy, etc., they just *do* these things.

This leads us to the most likely culprit standing between the person who does what she should, when she should do it, whether she feels like it or not (the success) and the person who avoids the responsible behavior (the "failure").

The distinguishing factor starts with the letter P. However, in this case the P represents Pressure's ugly stepsister: Pain.

In fact, pressure and pain are such close relatives that people are often unable to distinguish one from the other. It's certainly hard to envision any pressure without the associated pain. For instance, an upcoming deadline creates discomfort, unease and perhaps results in either real or imagined *pain*.

In his 1895 *Project for a Scientific Psychology*, Dr. Sigmund Freud presented his theory of the *pleasure principle*, which essentially says that as children, we are wired neurologically to seek immediate gratification of our basic needs, for which our bodies reward us with feelings of immediate pleasure. This is particularly strong as we move throughout childhood, our teen years, and into young adulthood.

Hedonism is essentially rooted in the pleasure principle, where pleasure (constant pleasure) is the primary pursuit.

Freud's Pleasure Principle further suggests that we are *primarily* motivated to move away from "unpleasure," or pain, and toward pleasure. Moving away from pain is more important than moving toward pleasure.

This idea becomes even more interesting as we observe the implications such a directive might have to your overall productivity and goal achievement. Just try to imagine a high achiever whose primary association with productivity or goal achievement is pain.

However, the fact is there are plenty of very high-achieving individuals, suggesting that everyone has the capacity to break through the confines of our natural, pre-conditioned wiring to establish new, favorable associations.

The more frequently we can enhance our awareness and redirect our behavior, the more we can forge new associations. Then, what was once undesirable and uncomfortable slowly becomes tolerable at first, and can even become comfortable, but not without intentional effort.

This idea helps to underscore a key premise in *The Habit Factor* as it relates to new habit development and the P.A.R.R. methodology. That is, by first **P**lanning, then **A**cting, **R**ecording (daily tracking plus notes) for a period of time (using recommended 28 days), then **R**eassessing, one can create mini-shifts.

It becomes easy to see how pain, or more specifically the *avoidance* of pain, is inclined to dominate our decision-making process and assume control of our behavior steering wheel. Let's call this tendency P.A.M., the Pain Avoidance. Mechanism, and if we're not careful, she will make every effort to control *all* of our decisions and behaviors.

When your house is on fire or a bear is chasing you through the woods, P.A.M. is not only our best friend, she's a real life-saver. However, when we are given the option to step up and volunteer for a school fundraiser, schedule an appointment with the dentist, register for a marathon, or just get out of bed earlier, P.A.M. feels it's her job to interfere, to take hold of our decision steering wheel. "Nope! No thank you!" she says. "We'll not be doing any of that today!"

P.A.M. lives deep inside what has been termed our lizard brain, and she has direct orders to keep us safe – to keep us pain-free – and unfortunately she has limited capacity to regulate her directives.[14]

Here once again we face a fascinating dilemma: We know that in order to improve – to become better people– we must grow and learn and fail and experience new things, processes that are almost always painful. Yet if P.A.M. has her way, she'll continue to interfere and *automatically* direct our decisions in order to "save" us from pain. In so doing, unfortunately, she impairs our growth – stunts our ability to progress and ultimately impedes our success.

This is where it is important to recognize that humans have a very special secret weapon (something that makes us comparatively unique in relation to other creatures): a much larger brain that contains the prefrontal cortex, a tremendous gift that (in most cases) offers us the unique ability and even the freedom to be aware (conscious) and usurp our "lizard brain."

When we take conscious control of this "executive brain," it affords us the powerful ability to craft new neuro-associations, to redirect thoughts and behaviors *after* careful consideration.

For instance, it's the executive brain (although some might argue differently) that allows us to volunteer for the school fundraiser. Or, it's the executive brain that initiates the practice of shaving or tying our shoelaces (carving new neuropathways and associations) in order to develop the new skill/habit.

An interesting thing takes place in situations that aren't matters of life or death (which is the domain of the lizard brain), and when there is actually time to consider, reflect and weigh the consequences. At that moment, our executive brain has the ability to *choose* – to decide to move toward those things P.A.M. would normally steer us away from.

Tony Robbins is quick to point out that people even have the unique ability to associate pleasure with certain painful physical acts (consider *50 Shades of Grey*, for instance).

The point, though, is simply to illustrate that humans have this fantastic capacity to alter and create new associations and meanings to any event, circumstance, person, place or thing.

A police car might represent honor, safety, assurance, order and civility, yet for many others, that same police car might represent oppression, violence and corruption.

Therefore, it's important to take inventory of those associations, and all the stories we tell ourselves about an infinite array of subjects. If these stories aren't serving us (by looking at our results), we have the capacity to rewrite those associations and create their new meaning.

WHAT'S MY MOTIVATION?

"You may not realize it when it happens, but a kick in the teeth may be the best thing in the world for you." ~Walt Disney

In 1919, Walt Disney was fired from the Kansas City Star. According to his editor, Walt Disney "lacked imagination and had no good ideas." In 1923, Disney was forced to file bankruptcy. Later in his career, after much success with Disneyland, Walt said, "To some people, I am kind of a Merlin who takes lots of crazy chances, but rarely makes mistakes. I've made some bad ones, but, fortunately, the successes have come along fast enough to cover up the mistakes. When you go to bat as many times as I do, you're bound to get a good average."

With so many failures *behind* him (an important point to recognize), a good question is: What motivated Walt to keep at it, to "go to bat" so many times?

Think about that.

I was enjoying a nice lunch with a very successful entrepreneur (as I recall, he had more than 1,000 employees in the commercial cleaning industry serving high-tech clients), and he wanted to learn more about The Habit Factor. As we talked (knowing *this* book was in the works), I had to ask him how he gets himself out of bed early every morning. I wanted to understand the motivation, what drives him to leave his comfortable bed in his nice home in his beautiful neighborhood and head out into the cold, dark early morning to (no doubt) tackle the innumerable problems of any given day.

I kept pressing until he answered. "It's hard ... it can be really hard," Jeff confessed. "I will sometimes hit the snooze button a half dozen times." I persisted, "How do you do it then? What motivates you to get out of bed?" Then he spilled the beans: "I start calling myself names!" I laughed. He continued, "I'll start yelling at myself if I need to until I get moving."

Marcus Aurelius, the great Roman emperor who ruled 161-180 AD, was an ardent student of Stoicism (Stoicism prescribed self-mastery via virtue as a means of overcoming destructive emotions). Marcus reportedly made it a point not to become too attached to his many available comforts. He was even known to sleep on the floor as a youth, believing that is what "real philosophers" did.

As emperor, Marcus essentially had any comfort immediately available to him if he desired, be it wine, food or even women.

As a Stoic, though, he recognized the dangers of being *too comfortable* – particularly how excessive comfort might impact his ability to contribute and serve his fellow man.

Marcus kept a notebook of essays known today as his "Meditations," and among his many musings was one about the act of simply getting out of bed in the morning (this is a translation):

*"At dawn, when you have trouble getting out of bed, tell yourself:
'I have to go to work —as a human being. What do I have to
complain of, if I'm going to do what I was born for — the things I
was brought into the world to do? Or is this what I was created
for? To huddle under the blankets and stay warm?'*

— But it's nicer in here . . .

*So you were born to feel 'nice'? Instead of doing things and
experiencing them? Don't you see the plants, the birds, the ants
and spiders and bees going about their individual tasks, putting
the world in order, as best they can? And you're not willing to do
your job as a human being? Why aren't you running to do what
your nature demands?*

— But we have to sleep sometime . . .

*Agreed. But nature set a limit on that — as it did on eating and
drinking. And you're over the limit. You've had more than
enough of that. But not of working. There you're still below your
quota.*

*You don't love yourself enough . . . do you have less respect for
your own nature than the engraver does for engraving, the dancer
for the dance, the miser for money or the social climber for status?
When they're really possessed by what they do, they'd rather stop
eating and sleeping than give up practicing their arts.*

Is helping others less valuable to you? Not worth your effort?"[5]

87

It's interesting how his dialogue includes questioning his own commitment to provide something of value to his fellow man as well as his own respect and love for himself. He arrives at the realization that there is an obligation to produce – to be "possessed" by some practice.

So, just for "fun," when was the last time you woke up before dawn?

When was the last time you did it 30 days in a row? How about 60?

To be clear, I mean get *out of bed* – not just wake up. Here's a terrific Chinese proverb that will perhaps help to motivate you: "No one who can rise before dawn 360 days a year fails to make his family rich."

Eric Thomas (motivational speaker and author) once articulated this message after a man asked him if he should sacrifice his wife and family for work or let his work suffer.

Sounds like a common dilemma, right?

Well, ET's answer went something like this: "If I told you to meet me in the parking lot tomorrow morning at 4 a.m. because I have a check for you for $500,000, would you be able to make that appointment?"

ET continued, "Not only would you be there at 4 a.m., you might even arrive at 3 a.m. Or, better yet, you might even sleep there just to ensure you wouldn't miss the meeting."

Thomas said, "You would do *whatever it took* to ensure that you were there to receive that check."

So the natural question is, "Does motivation come with a sense of urgency, or does a sense of urgency arise with motivation?" The beauty is, it doesn't matter! The two work hand-in-hand and that allows you to start at either end of the equation.

In 1519, a Spanish Conquistador, Hernando Cortez, landed his small force of approximately 500 soldiers near the Yucatan Peninsula in what is now Mexico. They arrived in nearly a dozen ships, and they were thousands of miles from their native land across the Atlantic Ocean.

Their mission was to defeat the Aztecs and seize Aztec treasures. Legend has it that upon arrival, Cortez made a declaration certain to capture his soldiers' attention. He proclaimed that all of his ships were going to be burned! There would be no way for any of his soldiers to retreat or to return home to safety. The scene became a literal "do-or-die" situation.[16]

Some historians contend that Cortez's boats actually sank, but either way, with no option to retreat, his warriors were left with only one option: to win!

And incredibly, against all odds, the heavily outnumbered Spaniards found a way to defeat the Aztecs.

This may be an extreme example, but it's worth recalling if for no other reason than to prompt yourself and ask, "How might I up the ante?" (Shy of dying, of course.)

Are there any crutches that can be removed? Is there a safety net that may be making things a little too comfortable?

Only you know the answers and how acceptable any risks may be. However, from experience, it's always proven a valuable exercise to challenge the story and the assumptions we often sell to ourselves.

To have a fallback position is nice. Although, when it comes to your real ambitions, goals and desires, a key question we touched upon earlier is, "Are you interested in achieving your goal or, are you *committed?*"

I can hear you now. "Look, I have a spouse and a family and I have a good paying, stable job. What am I supposed to do?"

As Eric Thomas advised, you're far more likely to find a way when you're committed to the outcome.

It's human nature to lean toward the comfortable and, unfortunately, it's a bit of a common fallacy to believe that what is nice, comfortable and stable *now, today* will continue for years to come.

In fact, that's the mentality former Intel chairman Andy Grove wanted to make sure his company understood, and it's an important theme in his bestseller, *Only the Paranoid Survive.*

A little panic (fear, anxiety on occasion) is not only healthy but is often responsible for survival and long-term success.

In the rapidly changing and competitive microprocessor arena (where processing power essentially doubles every 18-24 months and the prices are cut in half), dedicating enormous amounts of resources to disrupt the very business you created has become a best practice at Intel and nearly every other large technology company.

So, why would embracing change and challenge only be good and healthy for companies?

Success in business, as in our personal lives, is as much about mitigating risk as it is in accepting and pursuing risk (wisely). This sounds paradoxical and in many ways it is. Chances are you've heard the old saying, "Good judgment comes from experience and experience comes from bad judgment."

It seems that the sooner we can become *comfortable with paradox* the easier many things in life become – especially achieving our goals. You may not hear this too often, but it's helped me immeasurably: "Set your goals and then forget your goals." You set them to establish a long-term perspective and a horizon – a target to aim for. Then, forget the long-term goals and focus upon those daily behaviors (good habits) that will help you to arrive at those goals. Yes, it's critical to periodically check in and confirm that the original destination/goal is still the intended outcome.

The farmer has the goal of growing a healthy, abundant crop. However, his daily focus is upon the behaviors, activities and responsibilities that help to ensure a favorable future crop. (Notice, even in this example, a favorable *environment* is essential to a healthy outcome/crop.)

The longer we wait to enact such daily changes and set up that new horizon line – that new target/goal – the further out any new positive change can result.

You might be wondering (as Guy Raz, host of NPR's TED Radio Hour did), what in the world could possibly motivate a person to swim for 75 hours (yes, *swim* for 75 hours) in the Atlantic, from Cuba to Florida?

Diana Nyad was not only the first woman but the first and only *person* to swim successfully from Cuba to Florida (in her *sixth* attempt), and it was on her TED radio hour interview that she cited just one reason as motivation to try to achieve this goal of hers and accomplish the unfathomable.

Care to guess what motivated her?

Transcript:

Host RAZ: It's amazing if you think about it, this capacity that you have almost to be able to defy human capability.

NYAD: You know what I think it really is? I think it's the fear *not* of dying – I'm quite accepting of that – but I think that my <u>motivation</u> in feeling that tremendous <u>pressure</u> that <u>our time is so precious and so limited</u> – *that's what drives me.* That's what drives me to dream big and *not give into fears.*

(Italics and underline added for effect.)

I'm fairly sure this is how we started our discussion here in this book: with the acute awareness that if nothing else is going to force us into action (to press us toward our goals and new behaviors), maybe, just maybe it would be knowing that we'll be dead much sooner than we care to be (and that is in the best of cases).

In fact, it's that same awareness of the ephemerality of life that propelled Diana Nyad to swim for 75 hours across the Atlantic. And, perhaps not coincidentally, it's the same catalyst that thrust Roz Savage (rowing a boat) across nearly every ocean including the Atlantic, and it's the very same realization Steve Jobs had when he was first diagnosed with cancer.

Let's revisit Jobs' legendary commencement address (just parts) and consider these statements:

> "When I was 17, I read a quote that went something like: 'If you live each day as if it was your last, someday you'll most certainly be right.' It made an impression on me, and since then, for the past 33 years, I have looked in the mirror every morning and asked myself: 'If today were the last day of my life, would I want to do what I am about to do today?' And whenever the answer has been 'No' for too many days in a row, I know I need to change something."
>
> ...
>
> "No one wants to die. Even people who want to go to heaven don't want to die to get there. And yet death is the destination we all share. No one has ever escaped it. And that is as it should be, because Death is very likely the single best invention of Life. It is Life's *change* agent. It clears out the old to make way for the new. Right now the new is you, but someday not too long from now, you will gradually become the old and be cleared away.
>
> *Sorry to be so dramatic, but it is quite true."*

REVIEW: PRODUCTIVITY QUESTIONS AND ACTIONS

- How can I apply the formula Pressure=Force/Area to my own productivity?
- What is stress and how does it differ from pressure?
- How can you decrease pressure a friend might be feeling?
- How can we proactively manipulate the positive influence of pressure upon our own personal productivity?
- How can the intentional use of limitations and constraints boost creativity and innovation?
- How can the diminishing resource of time dramatically influence your sense of urgency and productivity?
- When is someone going to apply the pressure for my goals? WHO is it going to be?
- How does the inability to decide instantly diminish your focus and the opportunity for accomplishment?
- What is the Law of Forced Efficiency?
- What is your E to E ratio?
- How will the demand upon a resource be met by its availability?
- How can you stop P.A.M., the Pain Avoidance Mechanism, from preventing your growth?
- How can you alter and create new associations and meanings to any event to help reach your goals?
- What's *your* motivation?

Actions!

- ⏱ List a few ways to increase your "Area" to help diminish the corresponding pressure. Can you add resources? Extend a timeline? Identify an expert? List them.
- ⏱ List ways you can increase the pressure surrounding a current, important goal.
- ⏱ Apply constraints to a current project to boost your creativity.
- ⏱ If you are low on available resources, list 10 ways you can be more resourceful.
- ⏱ Add consequences and positive peer pressure to increase pressure around an important goal.
- ⏱ Prioritize! Identify the most pressing task and create a sense of urgency.
- ⏱ FOCUS! Isolate yourself from entertaining distractions. See how that concentrated focus pays off!
- ⏱ Create a false deadline for an upcoming goal-related task and see how that forces productivity.
- ⏱ List ways you can develop the habit of discipline.
- ⏱ Practice associating new, favorable associations to habits and behaviors that are critical to achieving your goal.
- ⏱ Recognize when P.A.M. is taking over, and consciously move *toward* productivity. Usurp that Lizard Brain!
- ⏱ Identify some paradoxes with regard to your own personal goals and what it's going to take to get there.

Be sure to visit:
ThePressureParadox.com/prism **for your FREE**
Pressure P.R.I.S.M. Assessment!

Performance & Pressure

Performance

"Pressure is when you play for five dollars a hole with only two in your pocket."

~Lee Trevino,
PGA Champion,
Professional Golfer

HARD DAYS ARE THE BEST

"Hard days are the best because that is where
champions are made!"

~Gabby Douglas,
Gold Medal-Winning Gymnast

This little gem of a declaration provides deep insight into the heart, really the *mind*, of a top performer – a champion. And, by the way the two (heart and mind) must be aligned when you are attempting to achieve your most significant goals. (The word "xin," according to ancient Chinese philosophy, translates to the idea of a "heart-mind."[17])

Let's look at Gabby's statement, given during an interview, another way: If hard days are the best, imagine how incredible hard weeks, months or even years might be?

Gabby Douglas issued that statement with a smile that could be seen from the heavens – an enthusiastic beam from ear to ear.

What makes her comment even better was the fact that it was clearly unrehearsed. It even appeared that the reporter was trying to rattle the inimitably cheerful Gabby a little, maybe bring her down to earth and get her to recount all the great struggles she faced on her journey toward becoming a champion.

The reporter started by reminding Gabby of all the sacrifices she had made: the missed birthdays, the family events she wasn't able to enjoy. "Well," the reporter pressed, "what about all those hard days ... the sacrifices?"

Who knew? Maybe Gabby might crack, cry and break down. That would make for dramatic TV, right?

If stirring a little drama was the intent, this journalist was barking up the wrong tree. Without hesitation, Gabby shouted back over the noise of the arena's crowd, still pumped up on the adrenaline and excitement of her victory: **"Hard days are the best because that's where champions are made, so if you push through the hard days you can get through anything!"**

No hesitation – zero regret. It was instant and automatic insight from the heart of a champion, only moments after her gold medal-winning performance.

It didn't seem to matter that the "reality" of her recent past was extremely difficult. In fact, only 210 days prior to the Olympics she texted her mom saying she was ready to come home, that she had lost her passion for competitive gymnastics and she wanted to quit[1].

Her mom, under Gabby's urging, had arranged for Gabby to live with host parents in Iowa in order to train with professional gymnastics coach Liang Chow. Take a moment to reflect on that decision and the importance of changing her immediate environment – to be immersed

---

[1] http://www.mylifetime.com/movies/the-gabby-douglas-story

completely in a new, supportive and competitive *environment where her vision of Olympic success surrounded her daily.*

Her relocation is a great example of what we reviewed previously in the Prologue and the "Three Circles" chapter, about how environment influences behavior and outcome. So here are a few questions: What are *you* surrounding yourself with? With whom are you surrounding yourself? What does your environment look like as it relates to your goals?

And how do you respond to "hard" days?

Do you become deflated, discouraged and dejected? Do tough days bring you down? Do you get depressed? Do you begin to question your abilities? Do you perhaps think, "Why me?" Why does life have to be so hard on me when it's so easy for everyone else?"

Recall Gabby's final sentence, "If you push through the hard days, you can get through anything!"

If you can push through. That's a big "if."

When life slugs you in the gut, do you respond like that classic Japanese proverb, "Knocked down seven times stand up eight?" Do you have the ability to respond to life with an "Is that all you got?" mentality.

Nobody is saying it'll be easy to do, but it is possible.

As a witness to both Gabby's performance and live interview, it became very clear that this young lady was coached and mentored to *reframe* all her setbacks as growth, as opportunities for future success. It was evident she was able to channel the pressure any setback threw at her in a positive way.

She essentially programmed herself through repetition (repeated trial and error) to appreciate and believe that life's daily difficulties were serving her intentions and actually bringing her closer to her goal's realization.

Otherwise, how could she make such a wild statement?

Do you think there were times when it was all too much – the injuries, the setbacks, the failures – when she wanted to quit? Yes. She admits that.

However, her overarching belief, mindset and mental framework (the mindset that literally and figuratively served her to claim a gold medal) was that each challenge would serve her efforts – *ultimately*.

She clearly had what Dr. Carol Dweck termed a "growth mindset," a mentality that understands any failure for what it truly is – a temporary condition.[m]

It's also worth noting that Gabby backed her belief with years of hard work, dedication and commitment, all of which allowed her to trust and truly believe in a forthcoming, positive result.

The other more subtle lesson we can gather from Gabby's response is that her coaching and mentoring encouraged her to focus upon two things, effort and belief, and to steer as clear as possible away from negative or fear-driven thoughts.

Now, recall the Pressure Prism from the Introduction; that image is designed to help us recognize the importance of *refracting pressure toward a desirable, positive outcome.*

---

[m] http://www.thehabitfactor.com/2015/02/if-grit-is-the-key-to-success-what-is-the-key-to-grit-part-i/

Sharing her gold medal experience with, *The New York Times*, Gabby said, "It was just an amazing feeling." She giggled, "I was just, like, *Believe*, don't fear, believe."[n]

So, back to you: How's the quality of your belief? How are you directing (refracting) the pressure you feel – toward hope and faith or toward fear?

---

[n] Compare Gabby's statement to the Pressure Prism (illustration) from the Introduction Section, "Pressure in a Different Light."

NO PRESSURE – NO DIAMONDS

"No pressure, no diamonds."
~Thomas Carlyle

As he stood on the podium after receiving the Heisman Trophy for being recognized as the standout collegiate football player of the year, Robert Griffin III (also known as RGIII) looked across the audience to his teammates and proudly thanked his family and his coach, saying, "This moment right here, it's unbelievably believable – it's unbelievable because in the moment we're all amazed when great things happen. But it's believable because great things don't happen without hard work...great things come with great effort."

"To my teammates I'd like to say thank you, and as we like to say, 'the hotter the heat, the harder the steel.' No pressure, no diamonds. We compete. We win. We are Baylor. Baylor we are, Baylor we'll always be. But it's up to us to define what that means, and this Heisman Trophy is only the beginning of that process."

RGIII could have mentioned any of a thousand experiences within his Heisman acceptance speech, yet it is clear that this idea of pressure (positive pressure creating diamonds) was so deeply inculcated within his mind/personal operating system, and that of his teammates, that it had to be shared.

It's also clear that these aren't trite mottos but formative ideas essential to the team's success and Griffin's development as an elite athlete.

As you might have guessed, positive pressure wasn't invented on the football field, a golf course, at the Olympics, or within the context of any other sport. Still, there are innumerable examples of elite teams and athletes who've allowed the pressure of intense competition to elevate their performance rather than destroy it. Kobe Bryant, current Laker great and certain future Hall-of-Famer, once noted, "Everything negative – pressure, challenges – is all just an opportunity for me to rise." While Kobe's initial assertion of pressure may be off, what is not off is his recognition that he can (and does) use pressure to his advantage as an elevating force.

As touched upon previously, there's a reason why at nearly every Olympics, particularly in sports such as swimming, new World and Olympic Records are set regularly[18]. If pressure were negative, race times would get worse as the pressure of each subsequent heat became greater. Instead, we see the opposite.

What we do know about pressure related to performance is simple: It can drive an unprepared person to want to flee, to escape, feeling nervous and overly self-conscious. Or, as Tommy Lasorda, Hall of Fame baseball manager, once said, "If there is pressure chances are you're thinking about failure and you're likely unprepared." Peyton Manning, future Hall of Fame quarterback, may have said it even better: "Pressure is something you feel when you don't know what the hell you're doing."

Pressure is not only something you feel when you don't know what the hell you are doing, it's something you feel when you've been slighted, humiliated, or perhaps when you've made a regrettable error, something that might lead to rejection or defeat.

It's a bit of a cliché, but how often do we hear about the star performer or uber-successful entrepreneur who was once the underdog, whose parent, teacher, coach, competitor or maybe even former boss told them they didn't have what it takes to become a success, only to persevere if for no other reason than to prove them wrong.[19]

Walter Bagehot, the late British essayist, journalist and economist, once professed, "The greatest pleasure in life is doing what people say you cannot do."

About a year ago I found myself trading youth sports stories with about a dozen or so entrepreneurs. The question was asked whether our parents watched many of our games when we were kids. While this was an entirely informal survey, I left the meeting a bit stunned by what I'd heard: Nearly every entrepreneur at the table shared that their parents were "too busy" to watch the majority of their games.

I recall walking away wondering (jokingly), "Huh, maybe I need to be watching *fewer* of my daughters' soccer games?"

What are the chances that those dozen or so entrepreneurs (me included) even to this day are still pushing hard on and off the field as business owners because maybe, just maybe, we are trying to prove something to ourselves, our parents, or the world?

The phrase "a chip on the shoulder" originates from the ancient right of shipwrights within the Royal Navy Dockyards in the mid-1700s and in North America in the early 19th century. The New York newspaper *Long Island Telegraph* reported on May 20, 1830, "When two churlish boys were determined to fight, a chip would be placed on the shoulder of one, and the other demanded to knock it off at his peril."

So whether it's being "too short," being cut from the team, losing in a regional spelling bee, missing a critical throw or catch during a game, or having the principal tell you that you won't amount to anything in life, or whatever your experience may be, there are countess reasons why we may carry a chip on our shoulder. Here's the key: Not only can this provide endless fuel for you to tirelessly pursue your goals, but the ancillary benefit may be even better: It strengthens your concentration, focus and resolve.

Russell Wilson, winning quarterback of Super Bowl XLVII and nearly of Super Bowl XLVIII, was drafted in the *third* round. He was skipped over repeatedly by professional teams and scouts because he was "too small" (at 5' 11"). Wilson admits to playing with a chip on his shoulder, "Because I want to be the best one day, not because I'm 5' 11" – for me it's waking up every day to try and be great, that's the challenge and that's the journey."[20] Head coach of the Seahawks, Pete Carroll, said of the entire team, "They have this grit about them that really could be called upon like it's a chip on their shoulder."

With a number of fifth and late-round picks and several others who were even cut from their prior squads, Seahawks team members shared a remarkable bond of brothers unified to prove themselves as champions on a championship team. It's one of the most powerful things imaginable: a couple dozen guys on a mission to prove the world wrong.[21]

I'm sure the number of famous and successful people who've succeeded *because* they viewed themselves as an underdog with a chip on their shoulder is in the thousands, perhaps millions, and the key takeaway is to recognize that each *responded positively* and assertively to their setback rather than negatively, passively or defensively.

So here for your edutainment is a very short and eclectic list of some enormously successful top performers, recognizable people who used other people's doubts and their own personal setbacks to fuel and inspire them to greatness.

Nikolai Lamborghini manufactured tractors in Italy in the late 1800s. The man loved to race cars and was a big fan of Ferrari; however, upon telling Ferrari what he thought the company could do to improve its clutches, they responded by telling him to "stick to tractors." That curt rebuttal sent Nikoli Lamborghini on a lifelong mission to prove his race cars would be the fastest and finest in the world.

Oprah Winfrey was just 22 when, after an enormous amount of promotion about her debut as a local news co-host and anchor, she was abruptly fired.

"I was removed from the 6 p.m. news exactly April 1, 1977," Winfrey says. "The general manager called me upstairs, and I thought it was an April fool's joke when they told me."

Winfrey continues, "And he said that to me with a straight face...I'll never forget the way he said, 'We're going to put you on the morning cut-ins where you can shine all by yourself'...As you know, when you're humiliated that way, you never forget."[22]

When it comes to your wellness, forgiving may be necessary but forgetting is optional.

After receiving his paltry $105 Social Security check, Colonel Sanders, then aged 65, was so upset that it *inspired* him to refine and sell his special recipe for his tasty fried chicken.

Twenty-seven different publishers rejected Dr. Seuss's first book *To Think That I Saw It on Mulberry Street*. Dr. Seuss then went on to produce some of the most famous and bestselling children's books of all time, *Cat in the Hat* and *Green Eggs and Ham* – both ranked in the top 10 by teachers to this day.

Even Thomas Alva Edison, good ol' "Al," reportedly went to formal school only for a few months before he was identified by teachers as being "slow." His mother then homeschooled him. Edison never attended any college, university or technical school. A prolific inventor and a man who left an indelible imprint on mankind, he filed his final patent number #1093 at the age of 83![23]

The man who altered the philosophy of science forever, developed the General Theory of Relativity, and won a

Nobel Prize for Physics in 1921 reportedly carried a chip on his shoulder, as well. Though Albert Einstein did not speak until he was four or read until he was seven, he believed he was going to unlock many mysteries of the universe before he died, and he was eager to prove he could. "He wanted to understand why the universe is the way it is. He died hungry, never having solved it."[24]

Even Demosthenes, the prominent Greek statesman of antiquity, suffered from a crippling speech impediment as a young man. Yet he found a way to positively use his difficulty to fuel his greatness, ultimately becoming known as one of the most famous and influential orators of ancient Greece.

From antiquity to current events and personalities, we find Carli Lloyd and *five* other players on the U.S. Women's National Soccer team who were each cut at one time or another along their junior and professional "football" careers. That's correct: Five women who found a way to positively direct the pressure of failure.

In the event you didn't hear the news, the U.S. Women's National Soccer team won the 2015 World Cup, and Carli Lloyd was presented the Golden Ball (best player in the tournament)°. Carli experienced a huge setback on her path to greatness – she was cut from the under-21 national team.

° http://www.usyouthsoccer.org/videos/one-on-one-with-carli-lloyd/ Watch Carli recount her setbacks and hard work as she wishes U.S. Youth Soccer a happy 40th Birthday. At minute 3:00, she shares a few thoughts on pressure – all well before the 2015 World Cup.

Carli called the experience a "wake-up call."

What did Carli do after she was cut from the team and got her "wake up call"? *How did she refract?*

Well, fortunately for her, her father sought out a specialist who offered to give Carli a thorough skills evaluation.[25] James Galanis, an Australian-born former soccer player and trainer, recalls, "We kind of designed a program that was to improve her skills to make her into a more technical player – someone who was physically stronger and someone who was mentally tougher." That was 12 years prior to being named essentially the best female soccer player on the planet.

Of the other players who were cut from their teams as they pursued their dream of a World Cup championship, Meghan Klingenberg (defender and midfielder) shares the almost magical power of positively channeling pressure. Still taped on her mirror to this day is a yellowed letter of rejection from her youth national team. "It will never come down," she says. "People told me you're never going to be able to do it. My stature, my size. As a player, I'm more steady than flashy; I'm never going to stand out. But that email is my reminder that you can persevere against the world."[26]

You can bet that every professional athlete, outstanding entrepreneur/CEO and certainly every Navy SEAL (as examples) has achieved his/her success as the result of the ability to positively *refract* and channel the mental, emotional and even physical pressures that beset him/her.

Chances are excellent that the most successful people you know and admire have overcome pressure-riddled trials.

Right about now you may be hearing a voice –a somber tone – telling you that your situation is somehow worse, different and more challenging. It's the same voice that may even try to convince you that you aren't strong, good, smart or skilled enough. Perhaps it's even a voice telling you that your goals are just too far out of reach. Why even bother?

In moments like these it's important to recognize who is crafting *your* story.

Who is forecasting how it will end?

Where are you putting your attention, intention and focus *most of the time*? (Recall the "Inner Circle" from the "Three Circles" earlier.)

You'd be hard pressed to find a "situation" more challenging than that of Hellen Keller. And yet she seemed to embody this idea of *positive refraction*. Somehow she understood the importance of directing the pressure *optimistically*, assuring us:

"Optimism is the faith that leads to achievement. Nothing can be done without hope and confidence."

Where does that hope and confidence come from?

Who is writing your script?

Who knows for certain how your story will end?[p]

---

[p] Recall these questions as you read the last parable in the "Mastery" chapter near the end of the book.

RELAX

*"The more relaxed you are, the better you are
at everything: the better you are with your loved
ones, the better you are with your enemies, the
better you are at your job, the better you are
with yourself." ~Bill Murray*

Aaron Rodgers, two-time Super Bowl MVP and future
Hall-of-Fame quarterback for the Green Bay Packers, had
this to say to his legions of fans in Packer Nation: "Five
letters here just for everybody out there in Packer-land:
R-E-L-A-X."

Rodgers reiterated the message on his ESPN Milwaukee
radio show. "Relax. We're going to be OK." The Packers
had just begun the 2014 football season amid high hopes,
but Packer fans everywhere were very uneasy about the
team's 1-2 start.

"First, people were impressed I remembered how to
spell it [the word relax]...I think when you say something
like that you take on greater responsibility as a leader, and
you take some of the focus off the team, and I think there is
a time and a place for that."

By "take some of the focus off the team" we can safely
translate that Rodgers was willing to assume more pressure

and at the same time try to alleviate said pressure from the other players and perhaps even the head coach. Football commentators everywhere were voicing concerns that maybe Rodgers was getting too old, and perhaps the team was on its inevitable downhill slide.

Rodgers continued, "We responded with a good performance…if we had lost Week Four it [the comment] probably wouldn't have gone over as well as it has because now we've won four in a row." In fact, the Packers continued their winning ways and managed a great run through the playoffs, making it all the way to the NFC Championship Game.

Can we correlate Rodgers' leadership and this one simple statement to the Packers' season turning around? Maybe. But what is more significant is the core message – *relax* – and its underlying implications.

It's safe to speculate that Rodgers wasn't just reassuring his teammates, coaches, trainers and Packer Nation; he was reassuring *himself*. Quarterbacks – the great ones – thrive in a pressure-filled world both on and off the field, and it's widely known that one of the greatest mechanisms to manage pressure (external pressure) is to relax.

During the waning minutes of Super Bowl XXIII, Joe Montana found himself and his San Francisco 49ers in a very tense situation. The team was pinned on their own 8 yard line and down by three points with only 3:20 on the clock. With the outcome of the Super Bowl hanging in the balance, and seemingly the entire world watching, what do you think Joe Montana said to his noticeably nervous teammates, in particular offensive tackle Harris Barton?

Legend has it that "Joe Cool" broke the team's huddle, and apparently the tension, by doing the unthinkable. "Hey," he shouted to Barton. "Isn't that John Candy?" He said as he pointed to the stands.

In the event you don't know, John Candy was a legendary comedian who, at the time, was at the height of his popularity and was, in fact, sitting in the stands.

Montana then marched his team down the field, completing 8 of 9 passes, and found John Taylor in the end zone for the winning touchdown with just 34 seconds left on the clock. The 49ers won the Super Bowl, and Joe Cool collected his third of four Super Bowl championship rings.

For the U-14 Girls Del Mar-Carmel Valley Sharks soccer team, their quest to win the Southern California State Cup soccer championship was more important than any Super Bowl. In one of the final games, after a tense half that ended in 0-0, the coach gathered the girls for what they expected to be the usual advice, adjustments and critiques. Instead, Coach Mark was quiet for a moment and then said, "Let me ask you girls something. Wasn't that movie yesterday *horrible*?" The girls were dumbfounded and some answered, with exasperation, "Come on Coach, we're playing a pretty important game here, we can talk about the movie later?" There was a collective, "What is *wrong* with him?" (Picture 14-year-old girl attitude.) The girls went on to win that game, and later the State Championship.

During the team's subsequent bid to win the U.S. West Coast Regionals soccer tournament just outside Seattle, the same coach attempted a similar tactic, asking his assistant coach to share a joke at halftime. For your entertainment, here's the joke:

A lady sees an old man on a porch and wants to know why he seems so happy all the time. She's noticed him there day after day for years, and he always seems so cheerful.

One day she gets up the courage to pay him a visit; she has to know just what exactly his secret to a long and happy life is.

"Well, that's easy," the old man replies. "Every day I wake up about 10 a.m., smoke about three packs of cigarettes, take a few shots of tequila and eat a half-dozen donuts!"

"What!? I…I don't understand," stammered the lady. "That doesn't make any sense." Then, thinking about it a little more, she says, "Well, you are extremely happy. Just how old are you anyway?"

"Twenty-six," he replies.

Have you ever noticed that it's hard to think when you laugh? It may not even be possible, and perhaps that's by design. Maybe that's how it's supposed to be.

Quick question: How self-aware are you when you laugh?

Laughter is known to decrease the level of stress hormones and at the same time strengthen our immune system. Laughter releases endorphins, which promote an overall sense of well-being. And, it's worth noting, laughter is even known to reduce pain.

Simply put, laughter helps us to relax and feel at ease.

When we laugh we aren't thinking, and that is a very important consideration especially when it comes to peak performance.

When I see a kid struggling on the soccer field – hesitant, slow to react, or experiencing consecutive poor passes or shots – I'll have a talk with her on the sidelines and, more often than not, say, "Stop thinking. Just go play, have fun, *stop thinking*!"

Once the game has started or the performance has begun, it's time to PLAY!

Perform.

Laugh.

Act.

Yell.

But please don't think...*too much*.

In the classic 1980's comedy *Caddyshack*, Chevy Chase's character Ty Webb (a golf great) offers sage advice to his struggling student Danny. In fact, it's become a very popular phrase that might be heard any day on just about any golf course: "Be the ball."

The statement is even better when you hear the preceding words: "Stop thinking, let things happen...and be the ball."

Cognition is a form of conscious reasoning whereby perceptions feed information to the brain for processing and reasoned action. However, when you watch any great athlete or great performer in any endeavor, they all seem to share a common operating principle: limited to no thinking, with almost zero self-awareness.

In any performance, almost all the thinking should be disbursed. The time to be thinking (the large majority of it) is on the practice field.

Baseball Hall of Famer and ex-Yankees catcher Yogi Berra was once instructed while he stood at the plate to try and "think while you're up there!" Upon returning to the bench after striking out, he groaned, "How the hell you gonna think and hit at the same time?"

Rap legend Eminem relates this very phenomenon in his movie *8 Mile* as he recounts the humiliating experience of "choking" in front of his own peers in a street "rap off." He overthinks, fails to perform, and then falls victim to stage fright, running off the stage.

In what you might call classic pressure-paradox fashion, Slim Shady (Eminem) then uses this painful experience (positive refraction) to fuel his aspiration to become a great rapper (recall "Chip on the Shoulder"). In fact, the lyrics to his #1 hit song, not to mention its very title, validate this one simple and key optimal-performance idea: "Lose Yourself."

The song became an iconic hit almost overnight and was the #1 song in the world for 23 weeks.[27]

A snippet of the song's lyrics:
"He opens his mouth but the words won't come out. He's choking how? Everybody's joking now... [a little later] You better lose yourself in the music, the moment You own it..."

"You better *lose yourself*."

That sounds a lot like he's telling himself to "stop thinking." Stop being self-aware, self-conscious; get into the music and the moment and just rap.

If you break down the lyrics further you may even notice he affirms his confidence: "*You own it.*"

In fact, what's common among performers – particularly young and less-experienced performers in the music scene (of drinking age anyway) – is the use of alcohol or drugs to relax and release any tension, to remove the self-awareness and the overthinking.

Rock-and-roll legend Jim Morison used to get pretty "loose," if you know what I mean, and it would make for some legendary performances. To be clear, I'm not condoning this tactic, but I do share it to exemplify the idea that relaxation and the absence of thinking (over-thinking) is a key pathway to optimal performance.

Peak performance might simply be defined as *your personal best* or even a better-than-average performance. Thus, the term implies a prior similar experience and/or an average against which to compare. Therefore, peak performance is a very personal experience and has little to do with comparing your performance against others.

If you happen to go further in the spelling bee this year than you did last year, it might be considered a peak performance. If you shoot an 85 in golf and you typically shoot a 105, it might be defined as a peak performance. You're likely to feel really good about the way you performed.

Peak performers and memorable performances tend to operate at a mostly unconscious, seemingly instinctual (or habitual) level, confirming what we often hear about the "unbelievable performance."

"She was in-the-zone!" "He was unconscious!"

For instance, when Stephen Curry, three-point shot maestro and MVP of the NBA's 2015 season, shattered the league's playoff three-point shooting record, fans tweeted in unison, "Steph was unconscious!"[28]

Sometimes this level of peak performance is referred to as "the zone," or "flow." The obvious question, though, is how can we try to replicate the zone or flow for ourselves?

An even better question might be: What core criteria (shared commonalities) are related to such performances?

It turns out that a person's state of mind ("state") has a lot to do with their ability to perform at a high level. A "state" refers to a person's psychology (thoughts and emotions) and even their physiological condition (how they use their organism – their whole body).

For instance, if I'm angry (thoughts and emotions), it would be representative of my psychological state, which is then likely to influence my physiology (body language), which might be represented by clenched fists, tight jaw, furrowed eyebrows, etc. The two – physiology and psychology – are magically interwoven, which means that when you change one you heavily influence the other.

Here's the best part: We all have the ability to intentionally manipulate our state whenever we desire. And, often the fastest way to do that is simply to address our physiology.

If I stand more erect, pull my shoulders back a little and lift my chin, it's going to be much more difficult to feel weak, insecure or unhappy. However, if I dwell on being unhappy (psychology), chances are good that my shoulders will slouch and my eyes are likely to gaze down toward the floor (physiology).

Tony Robbins (a world-famous peak-performance coach and strategist), who has coached many of the greatest athletes about this idea of "state" and NLP (Neuro Linguistic Programming), teaches athletes first to recall when they were at a peak state; by creating an anchor, the goal is to create the optimal state "on demand." Rather than deviate here about state and anchoring techniques, I highly recommend you check out Tony's web site and some videos on the topic (or even just his Facebook post on the subject).[29]

There is another key factor that predicates and directly influences a person's state. To my knowledge it hasn't been acknowledged (by name) *yet*. It's an essential ingredient to achieve peak performance, and I would submit it *is the pathway* to the zone. It's called *habituation*.

In scientific terms (psychology), the meaning of this word is incredibly relevant.

Here is Merriam Webster's definition:

– A decrease in responsiveness upon repeated exposure to a stimulus

Allow that to sink in.

What are the implications of this scientific definition?

First, consider that as a stimulus *decreases* during a performance, so will a person's thinking or, to be more accurate, over-thinking and self-awareness. In biological terms, habituation means "the organism learns to stop responding to a stimulus which is no longer biologically relevant."[30]

"No longer biologically relevant." That's powerful! Any additive information that is identified as irrelevant to the *goal at hand*, therefore will be ignored and discarded, which frees up available energy and attention.

Can you recall the first time you drove a car? How relaxed were you? How would you rate your first driving "performance"? On a scale of 1-10, how would you rate both the performance and the stimuli?

Chances are good that the first time you climbed behind the wheel you were overwhelmed, uncomfortable and even overly critical. *High stimulus mixed with being highly self-aware – thinking about a lot of irrelevant information.* You may even have been terrified that you might run over someone or get into an accident. You were probably hyper self-aware to the point where driving wasn't necessarily easy, nor was it much fun. *Low performance.*

Habituation fosters what can be considered the three most important and common traits found in any peak performer. Note: While there may be more shared traits, none of these three can be missing. Each is essential: **confidence**, **relaxation** and **focus**.

Today when you drive your car you are probably so relaxed and confident that you manage to eat your lunch as you navigate your way to the next appointment. (You of course wouldn't text on your smartphone or check email, though you'd probably feel relaxed enough to do so.)

You may even be comfortable applying makeup as you fly down the freeway at 65 mph. Not the brightest idea, but these sort of behaviors indicate just how *habituated* you've become to the driving experience, both the act (performance) and the environment.

Another fantastic byproduct of this habituation (familiarization and implied decrease of external stimuli) is creativity. How many times have you remembered an important task, or had some great insight while you were driving? Or, for that matter, brushing your teeth or showering or shaving? How many creative breakthroughs have you had while you were casually cruising home or to the office in your car?

The connecting link to both the *creativity* and the *creative performance* (driving while applying makeup, for instance) is *habituation*.

Such habituation leads to a heightened state of relaxation, perhaps even entering the realm of the unconscious or subconscious[q]. And, as noted above, that is precisely the point, since one of the key indicators of being in the "zone" is being seemingly "unconscious."

This may be why a professional comedian or a musical virtuoso might be able to improvise so masterfully halfway through a performance; their habituation carries them to an unconscious, creative state. The same can be said for the greatest athletes and their memorable performances – masterful improvisation to a point where the only explanation anyone can render is, "She was just in the zone."

---

[q] Such a state appears to foster superconscious creativity, as detailed within *The Habit Factor*.

While the car analogy is a solid example of habituation that almost everyone can relate to, it doesn't do a good job demonstrating peak performance because one of the key traits is missing: **focus**.

Without intense focus, it's impossible to realize a peak performance. So rather than imagine a habituated casual driver whose focus might be elsewhere, let's now envision a NASCAR driver travelling upwards of 200 mph, and you will quickly see how all three characteristics come into play.

Rest assured the habituated (experienced) professional race car driver will be **confident**, **relaxed** (which allows her to react faster) and, of course, *focused!*

While people might begin to think that a decrease in stimulus should impair concentration, it's precisely the opposite. When you are habituated, the stimulus is so diminished that it frees up your energy and attention, allowing you to apply it *where it needs to be*, thereby *concentrating* your energy with greater intensity (amplified focus).

Finding "The Zone"

Relaxed

Focused

THE "ZONE"

Confident

The Pressure Paradox™
© Equilibrium Enterprises, Inc.

Habituation
[Decrease in responsiveness upon repeated exposure to a stimulus]

What peak performers often say is that during the most intense moments, time appears to slow down.

In terms of habituation, this begins to make sense. With a decrease in irrelevant stimuli, the available attention (energy) increases and is *concentrated* upon a narrowed and focused area. Thus, the available data/information is magnified within a tighter "zone" (interesting choice of words).

Therefore, more data/information in a tighter "zone" could account for a time perception difference, almost like enhancing a low-resolution image and making it a high-resolution image (more data/information), or a standard television set as compared to a high-definition TV. Think about the difference in data/information between a 2D image and a 3D image. How much more data is displayed on a high-definition television?

Speaking of 3D, here's an even more interesting prospect: Since we already live in a three-dimensional world, what would happen if height, width *and* depth all spatially became tighter/smaller, yet the information increased (through intense focus) via a decrease in stimuli? It's not unreasonable to expect that within an even tighter area or "zone," a performer's perception may shift – particularly as it relates to *time*.

Now, we're only "playing" with theory here, but it's no coincidence that in physics the fourth dimension (also in theory) happens to be *represented by time*. So, the resulting experience for the peak performer is that she's so habituated – confident, relaxed – with additive focus (due to increased pressure) that her sensation of time slows down.

Now, let's put our attention back on relaxation and see how it influences performance another way. If you were to tense up your right arm right and hold it by your side and then try to move it in any direction as quickly as possible (keeping your arm tense and the elbow straight), what happens? Does it move quickly?

Try to relax the same arm and move it as quickly as possible. How well would a baseball player or golfer swing with tense arms?

Bruce Lee affirmed this observation, yet reversed the roles of the expert and the beginner and the corresponding results by noting, "Everything you do, if not in a relaxed state, will be done at a lesser level than you are proficient.

Thus the tensed expert marksman will aim at a level less than his/her student."

That's worth remembering...

R E L A X

As Bill Murray's quote from the beginning of this chapter suggests, relaxation, even as it applies to life in general, leads to improved performance in seemingly *everything*.

One of the surest ways to relax is simply to breathe properly; proper breathing offers numerous health benefits. (You can learn more about that here.[31]) Legendary golfer Tom Watson once expressed it this way: "Once I learned how to breathe I started winning championships."

If you saw the Academy Award-winning film *American Sniper* with Bradley Cooper as former Navy SEAL Chris Kyle, you may recall that an entire scene was dedicated to the significance of breathing and its relationship to sniper accuracy.

"Feel breath filling every cell of your body. This is our ritual. We master our breath, we master our mind. Pulling the trigger will become an unconscious effort. You will be aware of it, but not directing it. And as you exhale, find your natural respiratory pause and the space between heartbeats."

The essential components for peak performance are discernible: a psychological and physiological disposition that embodies a relaxed, confident and focused state – each facilitated via *habituation*.

When it comes to peak performance, the "Zone" is a special and coveted place. It's free from tension (think relaxed), absent of self-awareness (think confident), and demands intense focus.

The good news is the zone isn't exclusive to the super-elite; it's available to all – anyone who's willing to travel the long and often winding road that all the great performers must first travel – a road that is paved by...

(next chapter please)...

THE 3 P'S

"It's not the will to win that matters –
everyone has that. It's the will to prepare
to win that matters."
~Paul "Bear" Bryant

Performing under pressure isn't about becoming the next LeBron James, Carli Lloyd or Serena Williams – although it could be. It's really about recognizing that nearly everyone, at some point, can expect to have their "number called" in some way. When that happens, will *you* be ready to perform under pressure?

Here's the great news: Peak performers and peak performances are *created*, they aren't born. Sure, some people have natural tendencies to perform better under pressure than others, but nobody is born a peak performer. There's more good news: In most cases you'll have time to follow the "3 P" formula: **Plan, Prepare** and **Practice.** (I can't escape the "P's"!)

In a classic Woody Allen comedy, *Love & Death,* Woody's character describes himself as "the men's freestyle fleeing champion." So when *your* number is called, will you step up or will you flee? Here's an even better question: Which decision (stepping up or fleeing) will make you better, smarter and stronger?

It's been my experience that insight and strength are born from challenge, and when wedded to *reflection*, terrific pearls of wisdom are created. Aristotle affirmed this observation centuries ago saying, "Wisdom is an equal measure experience plus reflection."

Reflecting now on Eminem's painful rap incident cited earlier, we can see how it was only via his positive refraction that he grew and became better for the painful experience – not to mention the resulting hit songs, millions of dollars and, most importantly, a philosophy and a mindset for performance that the entire world could learn from in his hit song "*Lose Yourself.*"

As we deconstruct the 3 P's it's important to quickly acknowledge and understand a few guiding principles or precepts required for peak performance.

The first is simply that peak performance is a *result* and never a cause. Brian Tracy once communicated this idea, saying, "Successful people *are* the true price of the rewards they seek." Your performance will be equal to the price you are willing to pay in terms of planning, preparation and practice.

Nobody wakes up to find themselves a peak performer without first putting in the work – the hard work.

The second principle says: Peak performers *must decide* that they want to become the *best that they can become*. From my experience, very few people ever make this decision. This decision does not even have to be a conscious one.

One of my best friends was admittedly an average golfer, and one day many years ago he made the *choice* to become a much better golfer. Although he's stressed that it wasn't a conscious choice, he did say, after some reflection, "I was just tired of losing."

He certainly could have quit, but instead he began to take the game more seriously. His practice became very deliberate; he took lessons. He would also play the game three to four times a week, sometimes with total strangers or even alone. Simply put, he decided he was going to become better, and he was committed to that outcome.

With his intention set – to become the best golfer he could be – what do you think happened to his golf game after one month?

Not too much.

What about after six months? Eh, the results weren't entirely noticeable. Now, however, more than five years later, his golf game is remarkably consistent with a relatively low handicap, and his best posted score ever is a 71! A 71 was a score he couldn't even have imagined just a few years prior.

The third peak performance principle says: The decision to be the best performer you can be must be followed by a sincere commitment, dedication, and a consistent and adaptive effort. (Action, action, and more action in the form of positive, supportive habits.) The intention is to craft the required good *habits* that will drive the attainment of the goal!

To recap, the three basic foundational precepts and principles of peak performance are:

1. Peak Performance is always a RESULT.
2. Peak Performance is always a CHOICE (although it could be a subconscious one).
3. Peak Performance demands COMMITMENT, dedication and an *adaptive* effort.

Now that the underlying precepts of peak performance have been outlined, it's time to deconstruct and really understand the 3 P's.

The 3 P's Look Like This:

Peak Performance Architecture Stack
The Pressure Paradox™

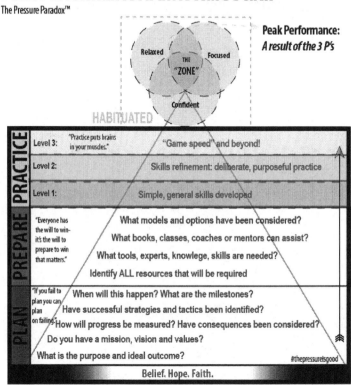

Peak Performance:
A result of the 3 P's

Relaxed · Focused · THE "ZONE" · Confident

HABITUATED

PRACTICE	Level 3:	"Practice puts brains in your muscles."	"Game speed" and beyond!
	Level 2:		Skills refinement: deliberate, purposeful practice
	Level 1:		Simple, general skills developed
PREPARE	"Everyone has the will to win— it's the will to prepare to win that matters."		What models and options have been considered? What books, classes, coaches or mentors can assist? What tools, experts, knowlege, skills are needed? Identify ALL resources that will be required
PLAN	"If you fail to plan you can plan on failing."		When will this happen? What are the milestones? Have successful strategies and tactics been identified? How will progress be measured? Have consequences been considered? Do you have a mission, vision and values? What is the purpose and ideal outcome? #thepressureisgood

Belief. Hope. Faith.

↑III. PRACTICE

↑ II. PREPARE

↑ I. PLAN

This is the staircase every top performer must climb and commit to cycling through indefinitely!

Depending upon your predilections for the spiritual and religious, there could be, and many would argue *should* be, a fourth "P," and that would be *prayer*.

Prayer, in theory, supports all of the other related P's. Prayer could help you better understand your purpose and planning. Prayer could provide strength and guidance during the preparation stage. Finally, as you struggle though seemingly endless training and practice, prayer would provide faith and encouragement along the way. Elite performers and athletes often say they rely on the power of prayer for many of the reasons stated above.

While "The 3 P's" could be viewed as a staircase or vertical "stack," the reality is that since peak performance is a process, the 3 P's should be viewed not as linear, but more as a continuous cycle where planning leads to preparation, which leads to practice, which in turn leads back to planning – and around it goes indefinitely. For those who wish, please insert prayer throughout the process.

PLAN: Peak Performers Plan

"Vision without action is a daydream.
Action without vision is a nightmare."
~Chinese Proverb

Coach John Wooden enjoyed saying it this way, "Failing to plan is planning to fail." There are hundreds of books written about planning and its significance to success, so rather than belabor the point here, we'll provide a cursory overview of many of the keys related to successful planning.

The great news is the act of planning makes you far more effective and efficient. There are even experts who assert that for every one minute of planning you will save 10 or more minutes in "lost" time. If that is the case (or even close), you would be realizing at least a 100-percent return on your time investment just by pausing and beginning to PLAN. Planning, in a way, creates more time and makes existing time more valuable due to creating a sense of direction and purpose. This is an important idea since time cannot be "saved" – it's fleeting.

From a pressure perspective, planning forces creativity, resourcefulness and problem-solving. The very act of planning creates constraints that are then used to direct energy with passion and purpose.

Whether your goal is to become your company's next president or build a dog house or a dream house, it all requires *planning*.

If you asked me to design a dream home, I might want to know why we're building it (what's the **purpose**?), what it should represent (what are its representative **values**?), and what it should **look like ideally** when it's completed (what's the **vision**?).

So here are some pointed questions to help you **PLAN**:

Why are you going after this goal? (What's the purpose? Is there passion?)

What does the ideal *vision* and outcome look like? Keeping a written description of the vision (in detail) nearby is helpful. Even better, find pictures or images; be as descriptive as you can with your vision and be able to see it with your eyes open or closed.

Have you developed a personal mission statement?[r]

----

[r] https://www.stephencovey.com/sample-mission-statements.php

The more clearly you can plan, the more understandable your mission and vision become. Knowing your plan will help you to articulate and identify the supportive values that will help to guide your behaviors.[32]

Recently, Jordyn Wieber, Olympic gold medalist and teammate of Gabby Douglas, spoke to my daughter's U13 Girls soccer team and recounted how she chose to miss her high school football games. This was a sacrifice made far *easier* because she was clear on her mission, vision and values. She knew her ultimate goal was a gold medal; therefore, decisions about how she spent her time became easier.

Planning helps you to identify targets, milestones, strategies and tactics that will be helpful in your goal achievement. Planning also helps you identify and understand the pros and cons of the undertaking before you begin. This is a very important concept – to really understand the sacrifices and the consequences of going for any meaningful goal.

Warning: As with almost all things, *too much* (planning) can be harmful. Some of the smartest people I know plan, then plan, then plan some more. I call this IID (Ineffectual Intellectual Disorder). This often very smart person waits and waits and waits for the perfect time to begin, believing they must have every possible detail covered. Unfortunately, the reality is nobody can ever have all the information that's needed. At a certain point you must TAKE ACTION!

Oil tycoon and billionaire H.L. Hunt once shared in a TV interview what he believed were the only two things required to be successful: "First, decide exactly what it is you want. Most people never do that. Second," he said, "determine the price you're going to have to pay and then resolve to pay that price."

THE PLAN

MY Goal:

_____

Target Date Completed is: _____

Major Milestone 1:
_____ _____

Major Milestone 2:
_____ _____

Major Milestone 3:
_____ _____

My ideal outcome is:
_____

The skills, tools and resources I will need are:
_____, _____, _____,
_____, _____, _____,
_____, _____, _____,

I will need to study and learn more about these topics:
_____, _____, _____,
_____, _____, _____,

What is the price I will have to pay?
_____

_____

Am I <u>committed</u> or just <u>interested</u> to this outcome?
(circle one) Initial here: _____

The five core habits that I could develop that support this goal are:

_____

_____

_____

_____

_____

I am committed to **<u>TRACKING</u> them!**[s] _____

(initial)

(See The Habit Factor blog, template or app, iOS or Android, about using the **P.A.R.R. method** for positive habit development. Link at bottom.)

How will I change my environment to support my goals and new behaviors?

_____

_____

_____

_____

How can I use pressure positively to help me achieve my goals?

_____

_____

_____

---

[s] Visit http://thehabitfactor.com/templates for a FREE habit-tracking form.

Identify five or more 90-day objectives/targets/milestones you'd like to accomplish to help you reach your over-arching, long-term goal.

_____

_____

_____

_____

_____

Other ideas, details and information you want to note here. What questions can you identify that will help you PLAN in greater detail?

II. PREPARE: Peak Performers Prepare

Proper preparation (more P's!) involves identifying all the necessary resources – classes, tools, books, people (coaches, mentors and models) – that can help to accelerate results and facilitate your desired outcome. In the age of the Internet there is certainly no shortage of resources to help anyone prepare for just about anything.

Preparing correctly means becoming somewhat fanatical about details and, like planning, it requires *foresight* – the ability to anticipate, to walk through and visualize a goal and recognize in advance any potential issues that might arise.

A great preparation and visualization technique has been termed the *pre-mortem*.[33] The idea is to imagine and visualize all the things that could go wrong. You actually make the assumption that things have failed, and then you try to understand why. Rather than waiting for something to go wrong, you *anticipate* all the possible things that created the failure. Then you prepare to avoid the forecasted disaster/failure scenarios.

Preparing involves being industrious, resourceful and patient. Consider Sir Edmund Hillary's successful attempt at scaling Mount Everest, which happened on May 29, 1953. He put in "years of painstaking preparation." That's correct, *years!*[34] Obviously, the higher the stakes (pressure), the greater the importance of planning and preparation!

Preparation includes identifying best practices while remaining open and flexible to any changes in the environment, such as new tools, technologies, strategies and tactics. It also means understanding the related risks and knowing what will be required to achieve the ideal outcome (diet, rest, exercise, stretching, etc.).

In many cases, preparing is a full mind-body and even spiritual commitment. Preparing typically involves research, study and maintaining a thirst for personal improvement.

Peak performers (because they've made the choice and commitment) often willingly pay top-dollar for the best coaches or consultants. Or, if they can't afford top coaches they will find a way to leverage that setback to become even more resourceful.

Recently, I had the great fortune of walking along the Sammamish river trail in Washington with a legendary performer, one of the greatest professional tennis players in history. A legend so revered in his home country of Australia that he has an arena named after him – Rod Laver Arena![35]

As we strolled along the picturesque river trail, Rod began by talking about today's great male tennis players Rafael Nadal and Roger Federer. I couldn't help but ask what he thought made *him* so great. "Oh," he said, as though the thought hadn't ever occurred to him (he's now 76 years old). "I was just fortunate to play my best when it mattered most."

I chuckled a little as I reflected on the statement and Rod's nonchalant demeanor. "Really?" I thought to myself. "I'm sure a lot of people would like to know how they can be so *fortunate*."

I couldn't hold myself back. "So, what do you attribute that to? Why do you think you played your best tennis when it mattered most?"

"Concentration."

One word – no hesitation. He didn't deliberate or elaborate, and unfortunately I wasn't smart enough at the time to follow up, as our conversation organically shifted to several other topics.

The following day, I realized my mistake. I had to revisit the conversation – I needed his answer. As I thanked him for his time and insight the previous day, I said, "Rod, do you recall how you'd mentioned that concentration was responsible for you being 'fortunate' to win the big matches when it mattered most?" He smiled and nodded.

"So, I have to ask you then, sir, what does concentration mean to you?"

"Preparation."

As perfunctory as he was the prior day.

I hesitated. This time I was totally confused. Honestly, I was caught off guard by his reply. I said a quick "thank you" and "perfect," but I had no clue what his response really meant. I had to sleep on it. I dwelled upon his comment for a few days. "Preparation, preparation, preparation." I kept thinking about it.

Then it hit me.

Of course! Preparation *is* a form of concentration.

Concentration means to "gather (people or things) together in numbers or in a mass" (from Webster's Dictionary). Therefore, the better you *prepare*, the better you are able to *concentrate*. The better you concentrate, the better you are able to *focus* (direct energy) upon your main objective, goal or desire!

It was *genius*!

Mr. Laver's statement cemented the second "P," an absolute requirement for peak performance: **Preparation!**

To best prepare:

- I have a plan in place.

- I've identified several resources for additional knowledge on the skills and performance objectives.

- I understand the desired outcome.

- I know the consequences and the price I will have to pay, and I'm ready to pay that price.

- I have identified who has accomplished this or has come close. What has worked and what didn't?

- I have identified the best practices, strategies and tactics.

- I have a list of 3–5 books to read to learn about the topic.

- I have researched thoroughly on the Internet.

- I have run a "pre-mortem" against my plan.

- I have contacted experts and sought advice.

III. PRACTICE: Peak Performers Practice (*habitually*)

"Practice puts brains in your muscles."
~*Sam Sneade* (*Record 82 PGA Tour Wins*)

Think about it this way: If practice puts brains in your muscles, how much thinking do you need to do once you have put in thousands of hours of practice?

Hence, a core premise behind why practice is so important is to ensure that it makes the slow *quick*, and the unnatural *natural*.

It's believed that instincts reside in the limbic region of the brain (the older "Lizard" brain), and when we develop habits our actions take on a seemingly natural ease and become lightning quick; they appear to be "second nature," and that is precisely the goal of practice.

This is why in the high-stakes environment of first responders and the military, they will drill and practice until behaviors become second nature (habit-like) and the requirement for thinking (during performance) is reduced.

Should a soldier ever find himself engaged in a firefight, the slow "act" of thinking might just cost him his life. However, with proper practice and enough repetitive training his ability to move instantly or seemingly instinctively (out of habit) is likely to save his life and perhaps others.

Just watch the top-10 sports highlights on ESPN on any given night, and you're likely to notice, for example, a tennis player who sprints to the baseline and then hits a perfect lob shot between his legs over the opponent at the net. How much thinking was involved? Better yet, how many hours of practice do you think he put in?

Similarly, when a shortstop dives across the infield to bare-hand catch a groundball and spins on his knees to throw to first base (which happens in about one second), you can bet there were countless hours of practice resulting in a performance of little to no thinking.

More practice = Less Thinking = Faster/More Natural *and* Better Performance.

Practice is as much an art as it is a science, so for purposes of our analysis we are going to review the three essential "levels" of practice and how <u>pressure</u> plays an active role in the value and success of each.

Level I: General/Broad Skills (Little to No Pressure)

Level I practice is for beginners (mostly) and emphasizes the component, general skills required where any particular, specific aim or target is left out. This practice level involves the simplification of technique combined with a general or "broad skills" approach in an essentially pressure-free environment.

A simple example of this would be to putt a golf ball for range (distance) repeatedly to get a feel for distance without having a particular target or hole to reach. Another example is shooting a basketball free throw without necessarily trying to make it in the hoop.

The main objective at this level emphasizes a general technique (stance, hands, and follow-through) to reinforce feel without the added pressure or concern for the cup or basketball hoop.

Another example of low-pressure practice could be an elementary school's fire drill. The practice is done repeatedly in low-pressure situations (without any fire, of course) until everyone knows exactly how to behave, where to go and what to do. Then, should a real fire occur, everyone moves according to plan and there is little to no deliberation.

A key to successful Level I practice is positivity, emphasizing what is being done well by the participant and sharing constructive and encouraging guidance. For coaches, encouragement is a key objective that provides a vision to the performer, showing that the objective/target/goal is possible.

Guitar lessons are another example. At first there is no pressure to perform, and expectations are set extremely low. This creates an environment of success, where the objective is to make the beginner feel comfortable and to become familiar with the instrument and have fun.

Since holding and strumming a guitar for the first time feels somewhat unnatural, even the most basic level of practice is designed simply to habituate the beginner to the parts of the guitar; perhaps learning a few chords to practice will encourage the user to want to learn more. Here's a great example of a SUPER basic guitar lesson.[36]

In these very early stages pressure is low and lessons should come in small doses, rarely exceeding a half hour at a time. The idea is for the participant to finish each practice completely encouraged, wanting to learn and practice more.

Level I Keys:

- **Little to no pressure**
- **High level of encouragement & fun!**
- **Short lessons – less than 30 minutes**
- **General skills like basic chords, shooting for distance**
- **Celebrate small victories!**
- **Simple skills games**

Level II: Skills Refinement (Moderate Pressure/Tempo and Intensity Increased)

Level II practice is for any participant who demonstrates basic skills along with an eagerness to become significantly better. At this level the participant begins to build upon a set of foundational or core skills, and then begins to layer on complementary skills so that one skill might feed the development of another.

This level of practice continues indefinitely as long as the participant is excited and encouraged to put in the effort and become better, refining their skills. Each specific skill is refined through proper instruction and repetition.

Depending on the sport, rest/break periods will vary between a day or two to longer periods. Typically, intervals of 2-3 times a week help to foster the repetition necessary to improve. Caution: Trying to practice proper technique from the outset is important, since repetitive drilling with improper technique develops bad habits that may actually set a participant back in time and effort.

Competitive athletes will practice most of the time at this level, since it allows for the development of new and improved skills that ultimately elevate their performance. Coaches and athletes use drills that involve moderate pressure most of the time at this level of practice. Occasionally, coaches will even create mini "friendly" competitions within their own team or organization using moderate to high pressure, such as scrimmages. Another example might be skills competitions among team members; for instance, a soccer coach may want to see who on the team is the best soccer ball juggler, or a basketball coach may want to see who can make the most free throws in a row.

Level II practice begins to take into account other factors related to performance: rest, recovery, physical training (beyond skills) and diet.

At level II practice the pressure begins to increase, and so does the stimulus. Therefore, the performer is encouraged to direct their attention and focus on things they can control, "the controllables," particularly when it comes to the performance itself. So, rather than expend energy on things beyond their control, such as the other team or players, referees, weather, etc., they direct their precious energy on things like:

A short list of "the controllables"

ATTITUDE
—Disposition, happiness
—Decisions, choices
—Emotions (most of the time)
—Coachability – willingness to learn
—Growth mindset

EFFORT
—Energy
—Focus
—Attention

PREPARATION (leads to concentration of energy)
—Diet/Nutrition
—Fitness
—Rest

The philosophy for ceaseless practice is summarized by one of the greatest boxers of all time, Muhammad Ali, who said: **"The fight is won or lost far away from witnesses – behind the lines, in the gym and out there on the road, long before I dance under those lights."**

Practice. Practice. Practice. And, more Practice.

Level II Practice Keys:

- **Mostly light to moderate pressure**
- **Encouragement & fun!**
- **Technique and skills refinement**
- **Elevation to highest skill sets and drills**
- **Increased frequency of practice**
- **Increased and varied pressure**
- **Internal competitions**
- **High level of repetitions**
- **Celebrate small and larger victories (personal and team)**
- **Building on the basics**
- **Mastery of the fundamentals – creating solid fundamental habits**
- **Emphasis upon the "controllables"**

LEVEL III: Rehearsal (High-Pressure Practice)
Practicing at "Game-Speed" *and Beyond!*

"I don't fold under pressure; great athletes
perform better under pressure...
so put pressure on me..."
~Floyd Mayweather Jr. (Boxer, 48–0)[37]

When the average Joe hears that Floyd Mayweather Jr. reportedly made $100 million in his fight versus Manny Pacquio in May of 2015, he's likely to foolishly say, "I'd get into the ring for $100 million and get beat up," as though that sort of payday was about *that* night or *that* fight. On the other hand, the knowledgeable fight fan knows that sort of prize is the *result* of years (more likely decades) of hard work and yes, planning, preparation and practice far in advance.

So, why is it that "great athletes perform better under pressure?" There is one reason, and it isn't talent. It is that the "greats" plan, prepare and practice better and work harder than everyone else[†]. Now, whether or not Floyd will remain undefeated for his entire career (he's currently 38, considered old for boxing), he'll still be regarded as one of the greatest boxers of all time.

A primary goal of Level III practice is to habituate the participant to the same intense pressure (and often greater)

[†] Some insight into Mayweather's training routine:
https://www.boxingnewsandviews.com/floyd-mayweather-training-routine/

of what comes with the "real" experience of competition and performance. This helps to foster the core, necessary traits required for peak performance: **confidence**, **relaxation** and **focus**.

Level III practice involves real-time rehearsals and "game-speed" practice. Sometimes it even involves handicapping or creating "desirable difficulties," for instance, tying a swimmer's legs together, or having a soccer or rugby scrimmage where one team has two or three more players than the other, and maybe even reducing the size of the goals.[38]

By making things more difficult for the performer – exaggerating the pressure or handicapping the athletes in some capacity – the actual performance appears easier. For instance, some high school girls' basketball coaches will have their teams practice/scrimmage against the boys. An even better-known example of this sort of elevated practice pressure is when Richard Williams had his daughters Venus and Serena practice and play tennis against young men. Today, it's common for top pro female athletes to practice against men.[39]

At Level III practice, the review of performance film is often used to help isolate issues in technique and help instruct athletes/performers. Identifying key limiters (constraints and issues) is essential; analysis at this level typically requires coaching competence and performers who are willing to accept constructive criticism. Peak performance is rarely achievable without a highly competent coach. Tennis great Andre Agassi has said as much: "No one can experience peak performance without a coach."

Interestingly, most top-level CEOs like Eric Schmidt (Google) and the late, great Steve Jobs (Apple) had coaches as well.[40]

The best performers/athletes/top CEO are not only perpetual students of their craft, but are highly coachable; this is because they have become *more* comfortable (not less) with pressure, have a growth mindset, and are open to constructive feedback.

Note: While a large part of this section discusses athletics, the parallels to business performance are not to be missed. You may be thinking, "I just want to present my PowerPoint under pressure to my coworkers and boss. I'm not trying to win an Olympic gold medal."

Assuming that you've already planned and prepared such a presentation, it's time to practice it…a number of times. The idea is to rehearse it at "game speed"! You ought to be able to present to a group or multiple groups of people, if possible, and gather feedback and refine and present again. The main idea of this practice is to "put in the reps" and become habituated to the performance.

And, if it were a presentation that could win you a promotion, the level of planning, preparation and practice ought to increase proportionally with the pressure. Therefore, to gain that promotion you would probably arrive an hour earlier, bring an extra projector or pointer, and maybe even have the slides printed in case there were any technical issues. Elevating the level of planning, preparation and practice according to the pressure helps to ensure a sense of confidence and corresponding relaxation and focus.

Similarly, if you were to pitch to a group of investors in your new business venture, you might even take your practice to a new level and involve role-playing.

I was leading a recurring entrepreneur group meeting a few weeks ago, and many of these ideas about the 3 P's, especially practice, were on my mind. I asked one of the entrepreneurs if he had practiced his pitch to raise money for his new venture. He answered excitedly, as though I was on to something. "You wouldn't believe it," he said, "how many times we role-played and practiced the interview and pitch." He continued, "My buddy would pretend he was the investor and he just threw every possible objection at me. It was crazy…we practiced so many times it was incredible!" "Then," he went on, "when the investor actually started asking me questions and he hit me with all of his objections, I was completely prepared. It seemed like I had every answer!"

It's no wonder he was excited: They raised enough money to launch his product and his company, and it's no stretch to say it was due to his planning, preparing, and maybe most of all his level of practice!

When Kelly O'Hara,[41] part of the U.S. Women's National Soccer Team, finally got the opportunity to play in the World Cup, she attributed her success to how hard she worked – in fact, *how hard she practiced*, saying in a post-game interview, "We have 23 amazing players on this team and I was just trying my best to stay positive, and every day going out to practice and working super hard and honestly, in *those practices, thinking this is the World Cup final and playing like it was the World Cup final and putting myself in that mentality*. So, yes, I was very thankful against China to have the opportunity to start." (Italics and underline for effect.)

By practicing (habitually) harder and faster than you may need to perform even when you compete, peak performances seem to arrive in bunches. That certainly was the case for Stephen Curry, who broke several shooting playoff records and affirmed in a statement about the speed of his practices: "I want to practice to the point where it's almost uncomfortable how fast you shoot, so that in the game things kind of slow down."

Jerry Rice, NFL Hall of Fame wide receiver for the San Francisco 49ers, was known for his "off season" practice routine that was so intense it became legendary; other NFL players would ask to join him.[42]

When Peyton Manning surpassed Brett Favre as the NFL's all-time touchdown leader at 509 touchdowns, Chris Collinsworth, NBC Football Night in America commentator, said something like, "Interesting, there he goes again, that's how you celebrate 509…that would figure, [after about 5 minutes of celebration] he's already preparing for the next drive!"

Peyton is routinely heard saying, "I love practicing *every day*," and he's known to be consumed by his "passion for preparation." At last count he held upwards of 24 major NFL quarterback records – that simply doesn't happen by accident.[43]

Very few performers can match Manning's passion for preparation and practice; however, one of them might be Michael Phelps. It's little wonder that Phelps has gold medals piling up like poker chips (he's the most decorated

Olympian of all time with a total of 22 medals), and it's not in spite of the pressure he's under, but rather *because* of it. It's also because of his intense planning, preparation and practice that has consumed the majority of his 30 years of life.

Phelps has so effectively offset pressure with the 3 P's that he says, "Swimming is normal for me. I'm relaxed. I'm comfortable, and I know my surroundings. It's my home."

"It's my home." Wow! Now that's habituated!

He is so comfortable, in fact, that when Michael Phelps jumps into the pool, rather than worrying about pressure, it's likely something a bit magical takes place. His surrounding environment (lights, cameras and the pool) all trigger a physiological, psychological and maybe even a biological state – a state where he is so comfortable that his conscious mind (stimulus) begins to shut down and he likely goes into his automated pre-race routine, *wired by habit* – a routine refined by thousands of hours of preparation and practice.

So, for instance, in the 2008 Beijing Olympics during the 200-meter butterfly, Phelps managed to shrug off a now-infamous incident known as the "goggle glitch," where water rushed into his goggles and he was mostly blind for much of his race, yet still managed to set a world record. Is that a testament to his good fortune, or maybe to the intensity of his practice?

Sometimes there really can be no precedent for a particular performance. Take Apollo 11, the first manned spaceflight to successfully put a man on the moon. There was great concern from NASA about *who* should fly the mission and concern about who could really handle such unparalleled pressure.

The astronaut selection couldn't have been scripted any better, according to space historian Andrew Chaikan, who commented in the NOVA documentary *First Man on the Moon*: "It's almost as if you were going to design the career of somebody who was going to do the first landing on the moon; I can't imagine how you would put together a better mix of experiences than the ones Neil Armstrong had."

The documentary shares a story about a preceding Gemini VIII flight and its serious thruster malfunction that seemed certain to kill the astronauts on board, Neil A. Armstrong and David R. Scott.

Recounting the Gemini VIII aborted mission: "NARRATOR: Back in orbit, Armstrong kept his cool, figuring out his only remaining option (to survive): disengage all the maneuvering thrusters including the one that was stuck, and use the re-entry thrusters to counteract the tumbling and regain control of the spacecraft. He had to reach up above his head and throw switches under this high-speed roll. That's amazing that he was able to do that, and he knew exactly where the switches were, exactly which ones to throw."

Fellow astronaut David R. Scott put it this way: "I mean, the guy was brilliant. He knew the system so well that he found the solution, he activated the solution under extreme circumstances [pressure], and I got to say it was my lucky day to be flying with Mr. Neil Armstrong!"

Chaikin followed with this, "That was sort of NASA's baptism of fire, because it was the first time that astronauts had really come close to losing their lives on a space flight. I don't think there's any doubt that the people who were running the show in Houston saw Neil's performance on Gemini VIII as a real demonstration of what he was capable of under pressure, in a crisis."

So, how could Neil Armstrong identify and throw the right switches on the Gemini (without being able to see them) in a high-speed roll? Was he just lucky?

In hindsight, what's really fascinating about Neil's experience on the Gemini VIII is that it could be said that it was his *level of practice* (including preparation and planning) that was responsible for him becoming the first human to set foot on the moon – an experience so unique it's truly out of this world!

It's hard to imagine a higher-stakes environment or "theater" than the battleground – war. Correspondingly, what is it that the military does literally around the clock, day after day? That's right: Plan, Prepare and Practice. The more intense the pressure, the more intense the response that is needed to address and positively direct the pressure.

The 3 P's aren't just a good idea for the military, astronauts and Olympians; they will serve the student, mechanic or businessman with the same assurance: The 3 P's always work when you do.

SEAL FOR A DAY

*"The greater the loyalty of a group toward the group,
the greater is the motivation among the members to
achieve the goals of the group, and the greater the
probability that the group will achieve its goals."*

~*Rensis Likert*
(Author and Organizational Psychologist)

About a year ago I, along with about a couple hundred
other entrepreneurs, was invited to train with an elite group
of Navy SEALs for a full day. The morning hours consisted
of physical activity, such as sprints on the sand carrying
another person "fireman style" (in a relay race no less!),
while during the afternoon hours we learned various
combat techniques, clearing corners (think home raid or
walking down streets in Fallujah, Iraq), and some emergency
trauma practices. There was even a weapons review
including a shooting drill (AK 47).

The day started with the entire group lining up on the
beach on a foggy morning in Carlsbad, California at 8 a.m.
and ended 10 hours later. Even as I typed some initial
thoughts of the experience over the following days, my legs
remained sore. As we huddled up, an officer explained the
ground rules for the day, which ended with him pointing to
a large bell hanging about four and a half feet high with a

dangling rope. "I can assure you nobody is going to die here today. However, if you decide this just ain't for you, that is OK; all you need to do is come over here and ring this bell real loud so everyone knows that you've just quit."

Nervous laughter rumbled throughout the crowd. And all I could think was, "that better not be you, Grunburg."

We were then broken into subgroups and given a taste (a very minute taste) of what the SEAL training experience entailed. From one drill to the next the message would be hammered home by the officer: It would be TEAM above all else.

For instance, you better hope you weren't caught conserving energy by not counting out your pushups or by not cheering on your teammates in the relay race. If so, you were being selfish – you were putting your interests above the team.

The officer's point was the team is only as good as its weakest link, and under *intense pressure* a broken link puts the entire team at risk.

The metaphor fits perfectly when you consider the very risky and pressure-packed mission of SEAL Team Six, which was sent in to kill or capture Osama Bin Laden in May of 2011. All it would take was a single weak link under intense pressure and the entire mission could fail. Credit to SEAL Team Six: Even as things went terribly sideways and the first helicopter ultimately crashed, they managed to keep their cool and execute the mission under intense pressure.

Perhaps the greatest trade secret of the SEALs is their unique ability to root out the possible weak links early, and thereby form the world's toughest, most inseparable high-performing teams.

The officer went on to explain that SEALs are often analyzed and participate in large research studies; millions of dollars are spent by business and government organizations in an attempt to deconstruct and understand exactly how these men are made and what makes them tick (and tick so strongly – *in unison*). He shared that the graduation rate from enlistment is only approximately 10 percent.

Near the end of our beach "experience," we were all asked to line up facing the cliffs (with our backs to the ocean). I was thinking, "Seriously? Another photo op? Come on, let's get real. How many more photos are we going to take?"

However, it got "real" very quickly. This was no photo shoot. We were instructed to lock arms and then walk backwards as the sand sloped into the very chilly 58-degree water, complete with waves crashing into the shore. Then it got fun. We were asked to sit down and then lay back – all the way back, shoulders on the wet sand, still with interlocked arms (elbow to elbow), all 200 of us, as the back of our heads hit the freezing, rushing surf.

I realized quickly that I was now at the mercy of a couple of elements beyond my control: other people (my teammates) and Mother Nature (the ocean). I recall wondering, "Who thinks this stuff up?" and "I hope a rock doesn't thump my head any minute."

As another wave rushed in and slammed into the backs of our heads, a few people began to panic, and an interesting thing happened: As the water rushed back out to sea it began to pull some people slightly deeper toward the ocean. With each successive wave we were dragged back toward the ocean by the collective weight of our teammates – still locked arm in arm.

We could not see the next wave coming, and as cold water washed over our heads I could barely make out what the officer was saying: "Only 10 more minutes." I said to myself, "There is no way we'll make it another 10 minutes." The person to my right was already noticeably distressed.

Clearly this wasn't a trial of physical strength, but rather a test of mental fortitude. Undoubtedly, the officers use this drill to filter out enlistees who aren't likely to perform well under pressure.

Thankfully, it turned out that his 10-minute warning was just a way to mess with our heads, and before we knew it we were told to go roll around in the sand up the beach about 30 yards and then resume our position back in the surf (all within 30 seconds). We did this repeatedly, and then later the same officer explained how this was "nothing" compared to the real drill, where SEAL candidates would remain wet for three days and nights while deprived of food and sleep – an unsettling vision.

The question was later asked in our Q&A session: "Are SEALs born or created?" The officer answered brilliantly: "Both. They have to show up here with the mettle, the basic ingredients, the fortitude and a mindset, and then our training is what molds these raw elements – forges them into Navy SEALs." This is not unlike the very symbolism employed by the U.S. Marines in their television commercials to recruit new enlistees – presenting a smoldering steel sword hammered under immense heat. Note: The forging is done under intense pressure. That is what galvanizes the team and the mettle of the individual SEAL's character.

Upon reflection, there were a number of great lessons from that day, and the most powerful might be this idea of the tremendous value of positive, constructive peer pressure and the crafting of a high-performance team. Now, I'm sure there are many men who didn't qualify (the vast majority), nor did they likely think that it was a tremendously positive peer-pressure experience. However, for the elite few who pass the test, there is no denying the positive benefits the pressure provides to strengthen the team.

Early on it was shared that each SEAL is instructed to look at the soldier standing right next to him, look him deep in the eyes and commit to him personally that he will not let him down *under any circumstances*, *ever*.

Now, strangely enough, one of the great motivations for this book, The Pressure Paradox, is at least partially related to where this experience with the Navy SEALs (and teams) intersects with The Habit Factor.

A little background: When our Entrepreneur's Organization (EO) forum, "The Rock" (at the time a group of 11 members), decided to utilize The Habit Factor tracking sheet as an accountability tool to help each member achieve their goals (via habit tracking), we all agreed and committed to ourselves and our "team" members not to let the group down.

In fact, we divided our forum group into two three-person mini-teams and one four-person team. We all decided that we'd compete monthly. The losing team would have to pay $100 for each member, and the winning team would be exempt from paying for dinner that evening. (The group would typically go to a restaurant post-meeting and play something known as "credit card roulette," which simply meant that the last card pulled out of the bucket was the "lucky" card, and that entrepreneur would get to pay for everyone's dinner.)

So the stakes were set fairly high each month: You could lose a couple hundred dollars or more – or you could save yourself from losing hundreds of dollars.

Perhaps more important, though, was the *commitment each entrepreneur made to his teammates* to follow through and not let his team down – to track and record his or her habits daily and email the report weekly. Each member's score influenced the team's average. (Note: This team "game" pre-dated The Habit Factor app; we all used the original tracking template and emailed our scores[u].]

Our entire forum would meet monthly, and we set time aside at the end of the meeting for each member to report on how well they performed their intended five habits (actual days vs. target days, percent). There was typically about four weeks of tracking data between meetings.

As each entrepreneur reported their overall percent, you could feel the energy of the group rise when someone reported a great score; there would even be clapping – often from competing teams. When an entrepreneur's score was

---

[u] http://thehabitfactor.com/templates

low you could sense the disappointment, yet there was a reaffirmed commitment by the entrepreneur to "get back on track," along with a rally of encouragement from his teammates. It was obvious that the entrepreneur was "playing" for more than himself.

For example: Of the five habits an entrepreneur believed were most critical to the accomplishment of his or her goal, they might report that "running 3x week for 40 minutes" to keep fit was at 100 percent. Another entrepreneur might report that his "planning" habit or his "use of three financial tools" habit was at 78 percent.

In retrospect, the "team game" of The Habit Factor worked well for a few reasons: clear rules, random rotation of teams from month to month, and clear penalties and rewards.

One month into our "team game" experiment of tracking and reporting, I was eager to hear feedback from the group. In fact, I was so eager I didn't want to skew the feedback, so I opted to secretly record the discussion. I really wanted to ensure the feedback was genuine and authentic.

What transpired next was entirely unexpected. The Habit Factor and "team game" were huge hits! The feedback was extraordinary; as each member reported their habit-tracking experience, the momentum and enthusiasm spread. These were already high-achieving entrepreneurs who were constantly looking for the best tools and whatever edge they could find when it came to realizing their goals, so I knew we were on to something big.

In fact, one of the more successful entrepreneurs of the group declared that he's "never tried anything quite like this." He called the results "magical." Another entrepreneur told the entire group that aside from the forum itself, "this was the most valuable thing he'd gotten from EO." That spoke volumes to everyone, because we all knew that our annual membership fee was nearly $5,000 a year.

I left the meeting elated; the feedback was far better than I could have imagined, and the value was already proven after just one month. It wasn't too long after that the iPhone debuted in the marketplace, and the group encouraged me to develop The Habit Factor app. The app became an instant productivity hit and, more importantly, began to redefine how and what productivity apps should do – focusing less on To-Do lists and more on recurring, core behaviors.

As obvious as it sounds, the idea of tracking as a peer group to create positive peer pressure via a "game" was only something we manufactured to "gamify" the experience for our group (in 2007). I had little foresight into the difference in effectiveness and even efficacy it would provide to The Habit Factor methodology.

In fact, this was the key distinction that led me to explore more deeply the environmental aspect (particularly pressure) upon human behavior. And, coincidently, it was about the same time that my business partner Edmon asked, "So, when's the next book coming out?" I assured him there was *no* forthcoming book. In fact, I was quick to point out that I never planned to write any book, not *The Habit Factor*, not anything!

However, the more I dwelled upon this idea of the Habit Factor having varying degrees of impact based upon the environment, I knew the subject of pressure had to be explored.

When Jordyn Wieber, the gold medal-winning Olympic gymnast (referenced earlier) and Maddie Jardeleza (University of Pennsylvania competitive swimmer) visited our girls U-13 soccer team, they performed another special exercise to underscore the importance of teamwork and, unknowingly, its relationship to pressure.

Jordyn and Maddie spoke at length to the girls about the value of hard work, vision and determination – attributes required in a high-performing competitive athlete. Then, the women gathered about 20 girls together in a circle and laid a rope down in front of them. Each girl picked up the rope, which was tied together (singular), and then was asked to step back. As the girls moved backward, the tension on the rope increased and the circle became tighter and stronger.

Once the rope was completely taut (and, interestingly, hard to penetrate from the outside), the athletes pointed out that when each girl was doing her job – putting in her share of effort and work – she helped to keep the circle strong. The women then instructed one of the girls to let go of her rope, and immediately the circle gave way, its strength gone. The once taut and strong circle had become malformed; it was weak and became visibly penetrable from the outside. These athletes did a fantastic job illustrating to the young girls the incredible influence just one member could have on strong team, and why it was so important for each of them to continue to put in the hard work – to keep pulling for the team!

REVIEW: PERFORMANCE QUESTIONS AND ACTIONS

- Why are hard days the best?
- How do you respond to hard days? Why?
- What are some ways to channel the pressure of your setbacks?
- What is a growth mindset?
- How is the quality of YOUR belief?
- How are you refracting the pressure you feel?
- Is pressure negative or positive?
- How can pressure affect performance?
- What is a "chip on your shoulder," and how can it be used for your greater success?
- How do athletes like Carli Lloyd refract the pressure of negative experiences and create a positive outcome?
- How does optimism play into pressure refractions?
- How did Aaron Rodgers' admonition to the media and fans to "relax" affect the pressure his teammates were feeling?
- How can you introduce relaxation in a pressure-filled environment?
- What is the importance of laughter in a pressure-filled situation? How can it be used to refract?
- What factor contributes to reduced/minimized thinking during a great performance?
- How can you move past cognition into a place of zero self-awareness?

- What creates peak performers and memorable performances?
- What is "the zone," and how do you get there?
- What traits does *habituation* foster?
- Why might it appear that "time slows down" during a "zone" or peak performance?
- What are the "Three P's"?
- What role does planning have in a pressure-filled situation?
- What are some great preparation techniques?
- What is the relationship between pressure and practice?
- How many practice levels are there?
- How does pressure relate to building a strong team?
- What techniques can a team use to enhance the positive influence of pressure?

Be sure to visit:
ThePressureParadox.com/prism **for your FREE Pressure P.R.I.S.M. Assessment!**

Actions!

- 🕐 Think about your own hard days; list three positive outcomes that improve the quality of your belief.
- 🕐 List a few ways in which you are an underdog, and let it fuel your motivation.
- 🕐 Practice an optimistic outlook with your own challenges; write your own story, envisioning the ending you want!
- 🕐 Practice RELAXATION when it doesn't make any sense – when you feel there is no time.
- 🕐 In a tense situation when you are with a group, try introducing a joke – find something humorous to loosen up the group.
- 🕐 Listen to Eminem's "Lose Yourself" a few times!
- 🕐 Use your physiology to stop yourself from feeling weak, insecure or unhappy.
- 🕐 Practice breathing techniques in a pressure-filled situation.
- 🕐 Identify your goal, along with its ideal vision and outcome.
- 🕐 Create a personal mission statement.
- 🕐 Identify the major milestones that need to be reached to attain your goal.
- 🕐 List the subjects you'll need to study and learn to achieve your goal.
- 🕐 Identify the five core habits you'll need to develop to help you achieve your goal.
- 🕐 Commit to tracking those supportive habits (daily!).
- 🕐 Identify resources to gather knowledge and skills.
- 🕐 Run yourself through a "pre-mortem" of your plan.

Peace of Mind & Pressure

Equilibrium

a: a *state* of intellectual or emotional
balance: poise
<trying to recover his equilibrium>

b: a state of *adjustment* between *opposing* or
divergent influences or elements

2

a state of balance between *opposing forces* or
actions that is either static (as in a body
acted on by forces whose resultant is zero)
or dynamic (as in a reversible chemical
reaction when the rates of reaction in both
directions are equal)

Merriam-Webster.com   2014

WHAT KEEPS YOU UP AT NIGHT?

"Don't be pushed by your problems;
be led by your dreams."
~ Ralph Waldo Emerson

A friend shared this quote with me the other day (aware I was working on this book), and while I like the quote, it got me thinking. What if RWE is just a bit off on this one?

What if there was a way we could *allow* ourselves to be pushed by our problems *toward* our dreams? Much like a Judo master, we would take the energy used to throw us off balance and then channel it toward an overarching goal.

Problems intersect our lives daily and ceaselessly, so gaining and keeping an intellectual state of balance or poise is never easy. Still, it can become easier as we learn to associate new meanings to our problems.

In 2007, I lay awake most nights thinking I was ruined. I was facing a foreclosure on an investment property and possibly even my own residence. I was caught up in the real estate debacle that engulfed millions; in my case, what triggered much of the financial hardship was that our company's largest account was a prominent real estate developer who was mired in their own battle to stay afloat.

While the crisis seemed to come about overnight, fortunately it didn't. Over the course of a year we witnessed more than 50 percent of our annual sales vanish (more than a million dollars). Bankruptcy seemed imminent and my near-perfect credit score was eroding quickly.

When I couldn't sleep, I found myself writing or working on our restructuring plan. What could we salvage? Where could we cut costs? We had plenty of good, paying customers and still had substantial revenue (unrelated to the real estate client); we just had to get our costs in line. Unbeknownst to me, I went through what in hindsight appears to be the "known" phases of personal crises: Denial, Anger, Bargaining, Depression, and Acceptance. (As related to the Kubler-Ross – DABDA model)[44].

Those tend to be the range of emotions you go through when faced with any personal crisis, such as grief, the trauma of losing a loved one, divorce and, as it turns out, even financial crises.

Looking back, I learned so much, mostly about the importance of keeping a positive outlook and *reframing* information (energy[v]), as well as not allowing my imagination to run too far away from me.

I did everything I could to keep my attention and focus on a positive, hopeful future and upon those things *that were in my control.* I did my best to not get caught up or waste energy on past events (that I couldn't change), or at the same time worry about a million possible things that might go wrong in the future.

"Worrying is like paying interest in advance on a loan that may never come due." I would repeat this quote

---

[v] Recall: The Pressure Prism "Pressure in a Different Light" chapter.

(attributed to multiple individuals) and remind myself anytime I caught myself worrying. I didn't know it at the time, but I was doing my best to refract the pressure – directing it toward a hopeful, positive outcome.

Would I spend the next hour or day worried about something that *might* happen, or would I direct my energy and focus in the present toward the things I could control – the things I could actively do that might influence my future condition?

Each time my mind would wander, start drifting down that unnerving and un-serving path, I would ask myself, "Do you really want to pay interest on a debt that may never come due?"

It's easy now to see how I was forced by the pressures of the moment to channel my energy *somewhere* – anywhere. This is an important point: The pressure *had to go somewhere*. Would it be toward a hopeful, positive and constructive outcome, or would I allow the pressure to be fear-based – directed toward doom and gloom?

The great Dr. Viktor Frankl, a famous psychologist and Holocaust survivor, author of one of my favorite books, *Man's Search for Meaning*, knew a thing or two about pressure – unnerving environmental pressures and human behavior. He beautifully articulated one of the most influential sayings in modern psychology, reiterated by thousands if not millions of people and then made even more famous by the late Dr. Stephen Covey (a fan of Frankl's work).

"Between stimulus (what happens to us) and response (how we react) is a space. In that space is our power to choose our response. In our response lies our growth and our freedom." ~Viktor Frankl

In that space lies our freedom to *choose*.

In that choice lays our ability to refract the energy, either positively or negatively. Recall the light-spectrum analogy: There is either high-spectrum refraction driven by belief, hope and faith (high energy/high frequency), or low-level refraction driven by fear and doubt (low energy/low frequency). Our choices determine which way we go, not the event/stimulus itself.

A buddy of mine challenged this idea about being free to choose our reactions, and his point was a good one. Still, he was confusing our automated responses to incidents or accidents (emergencies), where there is little to no advance warning, and our automatic, instinctual responses kick in. While there is little doubt that we cannot plan, prepare and practice for *everything* that is pressure related in our lives, for the vast majority of events there is ample time to become aware and react and *refract* accordingly.

As I thought about all the troubling events that could unfold, it occurred to me that I was in control – at least partially. How was I going to react to this distressing financial challenge? I could allow it to cripple me, or maybe I could allow it to inspire me to become resourceful and creative.

What I didn't realize at the time was that whatever my response *was*, it was going to be "right" – if only according to my belief. Therefore, if I wanted to believe I was doomed and it was all over, why should that be any more incorrect than me believing I was going to find a way out and be better for the experience? Which was more accurate? Believing things would turn around or believing I was going to be ruined?

Since the future is unknown and I could choose to believe in *any* future outcome, which belief served my interests? It stood to reason that on some level, my beliefs, thoughts, decisions and choices in the moment (during the crises) were in some small way playing a part in crafting a new, future reality. Einstein once professed, "Your imagination is your preview to life's coming attractions." Does that apply only to physics, inventions and discoveries, or might it apply to problem-solving and real-life ordeals and solutions?

If Einstein was even slightly accurate, I wondered, should I let my imagination run wild with negative visions or should I do everything in my power to craft a hopeful, positive image of the future?

I clearly recall two significant phone calls on a particularly dark, depressing and brutal day. It appeared that we would be closing our business by month's end – there was just too much loss, too much debt; it all seemed fairly hopeless.

Looking back now, it's easy to see how it was the proverbial "darkest hour before the dawn" type scenario. My long-time business partner said, "Martin, what are *you* going to do? I'm not sure if we're going to be here in two or three months." He was being very generous in his estimate knowing that we might be closing our doors at the end of the month.

My reply came semi-automatically and caught me off guard as it came out of my mouth. "It's OK, I understand." (I had a very strange sense of calm, finding myself trying to ease *his* worries about me and my family). All I had to offer was, "I get it, I understand, we'll be alright. At this point – now, today, this moment," I assured him and myself, "we are still in business. So, I'm just going to take it one day at a time."

One day at a time.

The interesting thing is once you become willing to accept the worst possible outcome involving factors that are beyond your control, you tend to have an immediate feeling of peace.

I didn't know this at the time, but Carl Jung's observation helps to shed light on this: "What you resist," he said "persists." By constantly fighting and resisting the negative thought of bankruptcy or foreclosure, it remained ever-present; it remained at the forefront of my mind. It became all-encompassing and the fear was crippling.

However, as soon as I let that thought go and actually surrendered (which doesn't mean giving up) to the *possibility* of foreclosure and bankruptcy, by acknowledging that they could happen and coming to terms with those outcomes, the fear subsided immediately.

A prolific Chinese author, Lin Yutang, put it this way: "Peace of mind is that mental condition in which you have accepted the worst."

What's interesting to consider is that, ultimately, the "worst" case in any situation is truly our ultimate fear – death.

There is a terrific parable about a Samurai warrior and a Tea Master that underscores this awareness. The short story goes something like this:

There once was a Tea Master who served many great Samurai warriors, and in his part of Japan it was acceptable for him to wear clothes similar to those of the mighty Samurai.

One day, however, upon travels to another part of Japan, the Tea Master came upon a different group of Samurai who took offense to his dress. The Tea Master was small and scrawny, and one particular Samurai became so offended by this poor imitation of a Samurai, he felt he must challenge the Tea Master to a dual – explaining that the Tea Master either would die like a real warrior or a dog, but either way he wouldn't be around to further misrepresent the great Samurai warrior.

Immediately, the Tea Master became faint and a little ill, and then he grew weak. His friends tried to comfort him and even help him to raise money with the hope that they could bribe the Samurai out of the upcoming duel.

However, as the evening before his battle approached, the Tea Master sought out a local Zen Master. "Please, Master, I want to know how I can die like a real warrior – like a true Samurai?"

"Prepare my tea!" demanded the Zen Master in response.

Confused, the Tea Master began his tea ceremony, serenely preparing the tea, greeting the Zen Master with a bow, and serving him with great pride.

"That," the Zen Master explained, "is precisely how you should address the Samurai warrior tomorrow morning. I want you to act as though you are about to serve him tea instead of going to combat. You must be confident, focused and also relaxed – even serene. Be sure you greet him warmly and salute him courteously. Remain calm. You might even suggest that you wish he showed up a little earlier, as you have been very eager to see him.

"Then, after a warm and friendly greeting, I want you to raise your sword high with immense pride and hold it above your head sturdy and confident. Be sure to look him square in the eye – then prepare yourself for battle!"

The next morning the Tea Master did just as instructed. He rose early and awaited the Samurai's entrance. He had a calm, confident disposition; he greeted the Samurai with great respect and inner strength. When the time came, he wrapped his scarf around his forehead and, with a slight smile and accepting of the worst possible outcome, he calmly and confidently raised his sword high above his head, ready for battle, precisely as the Zen Master advised.

The Samurai warrior was immediately confused. He'd been expecting a quivering little heap of a man. Then, he began to wonder if he had been tricked. "What is going on here?" he thought. "Where is that cowering little Tea Merchant?"

Recognizing his time was running short, the Samurai became terrified; it occurred to him that even in the best-case scenario it was likely that they both would die – something he had never anticipated. There was only one thing the Samurai could do to spare his own life. He quickly bowed to the Tea Master and asked for forgiveness. Further, he apologized for his rude behavior, and with permission left the area as quickly as possible.

Ironically, it was the Tea Master's acceptance of his own fate and possible death (not its resistance) that gave him great strength, confidence, and the inner peace required to march into battle.

It is with a similar acceptance of our own circumstance and fate (whatever it may be) that we can shift our mindset from resistance to acceptance – to embrace the circumstances we cannot control rather than fight them. By doing this we conserve a great deal of energy that can be positively channeled in new directions. Such an accepting mindset also brings about a sense of calm, renewed peace of mind, and a tremendous appreciation for the *present*.

Back to my 2007 financial crisis. I received a phone call from a long-time friend just a few hours after I'd spoken to my business partner. The voicemail said, "Just checking in on you buddy. I'm a little worried about you ... whatever you need, my sense is things are really tough on you right now. Listen, if you need anything, please let me know."

I returned his call a bit later and my statement remained strangely consistent. "Thanks, that means a lot." Taking count of my blessings, I continued, "I'm OK – everyone is healthy and we're all just taking things *one day at a time*."

We're just taking things one day at a time.

Month after month I would draw whatever was necessary from a dwindling IRA account – the savings had vanished.

It was one of the most challenging and resourceful times of my life. Awake many nights, I would consciously *redirect my energy* toward some of my creative endeavors: writing, blogging and app development. I felt that applying my focus and attention to creative projects was also a way to "trust" in so many factors and outcomes far beyond my control.

Strangely, and probably worth noting, during that period – amidst all the chaos – I was probably the most creative and physically fit I had been in years. On the surface this doesn't make much sense. I now recognize it was my way to try to attain a sense of equilibrium.

Amid all the uncertainly, of all things, I signed up for an Ironman triathlon. I reasoned that such a commitment would help to forge better habits (diet, exercise – and I tracked them daily). I even made time for recreation, coaching soccer, surfing, running, and traveling (if I could creatively finance it). All these extracurricular activities, it turned out, helped to offset the enormous pressures of the time.

Another powerful gift of going through a trying time is that the noise on the periphery tends to fade. Things that appeared to matter really didn't, whether it was a sports team, a new tech gadget or something on social media. Those concerns all subsided. Perhaps the best gift of all is that you're immediately reminded of who your real friends are, and how fortunate you are to have family and friends who will rally to support you during tough times.[w]

It turns out there was a strange type of beauty amid all the chaos, and it became more apparent *because of* the difficult times: All those "free" things – health, family and friends – are truly *priceless*.

---

[w] Enhancing our "Surface Area"!

THE GREATEST GENERATION

"It is, I believe, the greatest generation any society has ever produced."
~*Tom Brokaw*

How much reverse engineering might we need to understand exactly how and why "The Greatest Generation" was attributed such a moniker?

What made them so "great"?

Take a moment to reflect upon the immense pressures of the time and the enormous sacrifices this generation must have endured.

This generation was book-ended by the Great Depression and World War II – two horrific events you might not wish upon your worst enemy. And yet, what emerged from the ashes of the war to end all wars? A personality type that was resolute and refined, softened by humility and great compassion, yet hardened by unimaginable atrocities. They possessed a disposition so easy to distinguish, in fact, they've simply become known as the Greatest Generation.

A bit romantic, perhaps, but there is little denying the *positive* influence the generation has had as well as the many great achievements and personalities that arose during this period.

Does that mean we all need to go suffer a cataclysmic event like a World War or Great Depression in order to refine our character? I certainly hope not. But what it does suggest is that we can learn a lot about the human condition – its ability to properly respond, adapt and evolve to deal with unimaginable pressures.

Next let's consider the 1700s, another very difficult period, and the distinguished men known as our "founding fathers." During that time, just to travel a few miles could take an hour or more by horseback or carriage. They didn't have the modern comforts of society, such as electricity, airline travel and automobiles, and certainly not the productivity tools we take for granted – the Internet, search engines, smartphones, computers, printers, calendaring and email software, online conferencing tools, etc. Still, what they were able to overcome and create is remarkable.

If you were to analyze both periods and their corresponding prolific personalities, an undeniable theme arises. First, under overwhelming pressure the representative characters found a way to direct (refract) pressure toward a positive, hopeful outcome. Second, they were operating with an enormous sense of *purpose*!

You may wonder, for instance, what George Washington could be thinking in the midst of the Revolutionary War – a war unprecedented at that time in human history. The good news is General Washington wrote a number of letters, so we are granted unique insight into the thoughts of a man who has long been regarded as one of the greatest leaders in human history.

On one of the more challenging days of the Revolution, October 27, 1777, Washington wrote to Landon Carter: "I flatter myself that a superintending Providence is ordering everything for the best and that, in due time, all will end well."[45] A few months later, on December 31 of the same year, he writes to Marquis de Lafayette: "I have no doubt but that everything happens so for the best; that we shall triumph over all our misfortunes and shall, in the end, be ultimately happy."[46]

Amid complete uncertainty and enormous pressure, General George Washington could have chosen to believe both he and his forces were doomed – matched up against a better-equipped army. After all, they had already been defeated, losing New York City and New Jersey earlier in the war. Yet, as he wrote this letter he chose to believe and to refract the pressures of the moment toward a positive outcome.

Here's the key: General Washington had little if any available information to support his belief. However, when it came to having a purpose, it's hard to imagine a more significant one: to overthrow King George III and the British Empire and to establish democracy in a free land – a government for and by the people.

Now, try to imagine the intensity of purpose the Allies felt during World War II when confronting the Nazis, in particular Great Britain and Sir Winston Churchill. As he addressed his country, Churchill underscored his faith in the British troops and so enlarged their purpose as to imply that the entire world's freedom hung in the balance – immense pressure matched by unwavering purpose!

On June 18, 1940, Churchill declared the following as part of his "Their Finest Hour" speech:

> "Hitler knows that he will have to break us in this Island or lose the war. If we can stand up to him, all Europe may be free and the life of the world may move forward into broad, sunlit uplands. But if we fail, then the whole world, including the United States, including all that we have known and cared for, will sink into the abyss of a new Dark Age made more sinister, and perhaps more protracted, by the lights of perverted science.
> Let us therefore brace ourselves to our duties, and so bear ourselves that if the British Empire and its Commonwealth last for a thousand years, men will still say, 'This was their finest hour.'"

Later, as the Nazis' bombs rained down across Europe, Churchill paid a visit to the U.S. Congress on December 26, 1941. Still under immense uncertainty and unimaginable pressure, his optimism and purpose remained resolute and impossible to ignore.

> "Whether deliverance comes in 1942 or 1943 or 1944, falls into its proper place in the grand proportions of human history. Sure I am that this day, now, we are the masters of our fate. That the task which has been set us is not above our strength. That its pangs and toils are not beyond our endurance. As long as we have faith in our cause, and an unconquerable willpower, salvation will not be denied us."[47]

With the understanding that pressure (energy) must go somewhere, and that we have the power to direct it, it's essential to understand the significance that *purpose* plays in the positive refraction of pressure: Purpose greatly facilitates the positive application of pressure. In fact, Brazilian soccer great Neymar Jr. once noted, "There is <u>no pressure</u> when you are making your dreams come true." *That's purpose!*

It's almost cliché to hear about the single mother of four who, despite working three part-time jobs, finds a way to raise, feed and clothe all her kids, and to put them through school and make sure they all graduate.

Future NBA Hall of Famer Kevin Durant said as much during his tear-jerking acceptance speech as he received the 2013-14 season MVP award.

"And last my mom. We weren't supposed to be here. You made us *believe*. You kept us off the street. You put clothes on our backs, food on the table. When you didn't eat, you made sure we ate. You went to sleep hungry. You sacrificed for us. You're the real MVP[x]."

Returning to the Greatest Generation, here's a thought: What if we were to compare and contrast generations? For instance, Gen X, Gen Y, the Millennials (or pick any generation) versus The Greatest Generation? How might the others stack up?

"Who cares? What's the point?" I can hear some readers ask (particularly the younger ones).

---

[x] Watch this video! http://www.washingtonpost.com/blogs/post-partisan/wp/2014/05/07/kevin-durant-praises-the-real-mvp/

While every generation is sure to have its unique strengths, it's hard to argue that any might have more "grit" than the Greatest Generation.

What's the point? According to Angela Lee Duckworth,[48] "grit" is a distinguishing characteristic of those who succeed. And, according to her research, it's more important than other factors commonly believed to predicate success, such as IQ, talent or where you go to college."[49]

To be gritty means you willingly engage in a long-term effort to see your goal to fruition (purpose). It means that you persist, adapt and commit to an outcome. A gritty person recognizes that it may take years, decades or even longer to ultimately "succeed." (Duckworth cites a couple of characters we've already mentioned, Steve Jobs and Abraham Lincoln, as examples of gritty characters.)

Furthermore, a gritty person recognizes life as a continuous opportunity for growth. In fact, continuous growth *is* the overarching goal. Technically, then, you never "arrive." This is the essence of the "journey" versus "destination" mentality.

Grit simply might be known as a "super-trait" whose key attributes include responsibility, resolve, resourcefulness and resilience (the 4 R's). In total, they are precisely the traits that characterize the Greatest Generation in its purest form.

This an important word to contemplate: **character**-*ize*. The Latin root of the word habit is *habit-us*, and in its simplest form means "condition" and/or "character." We must understand that our condition (now) at this moment, and our character (how we are known to be), is the sum total result of all our habits (thought and behavior) up to this moment in time.

Therefore, grit and its related sub-traits are all positive habits that can be developed just like any other habit. Nobody, it turns out, is born gritty, resourceful or disciplined.

The great news is you have the ability to craft these habits intentionally any time you desire. It's helpful to think about it this way: Good habits happen when planned; bad habits happen on their own.[y]

Here's another important point: The Greatest Generation had grit in spades *because* of the ceaseless challenges that beset them. Grit for them was the result of an environment that produced nearly constant pressure; therefore, the vast majority of these characters couldn't help but forge the essential habits that make up grit.

The math is fairly simple: No pressure, no grit!

"That sucks!" I can hear someone say. "You mean I need to be gritty to become successful, and I must have problems to become gritty? But, I don't like problems!"

It's a conundrum that reminds me of a great song by Johnny Cash titled "A Boy Named Sue."[50] The gist of the song is that a deadbeat dad comes to the realization that his son (without a father) is going to have a tough road ahead,

---

[y] For more insight on how to intentionally craft good habits using P.A.R.R. methodology, watch this new video:
https://www.youtube.com/watch?v=sJIJVJiwvMo

and he wants to make sure his son is tough. So, in order to ensure he's extra-tough, the dad names his son Sue.

Here's just a snippet of the song's lyrics:

Son, this world is rough
And if a man's gonna make it, he's gotta be tough
And I knew I wouldn't be there to help ya along.
So I give ya that name and I said goodbye
I knew you'd have to get tough or die
And it's the name that helped to make you strong.

Now, having said all that, if you still don't want any problems in your life (and I can't blame you, since it sounds very appealing), I do know of one very special place that is free from all problems and all worry. A quick warning: It's a bit of a solemn and quiet place, but there really isn't a care in the world – and you can be sure there is zero pressure.

Where do you think such a magical place exists? [z]

---

[z] The cemetery.

SEEKING EQUILIBRIUM

"Set peace of mind as your highest goal and organize your life around it."

Brian Tracy

God, if she exists, must have a terrific sense of humor. Consider that as infants, we (humans) are pre-wired to seek pleasure and avoid pain (Freud's pleasure principle in action). However, if this behavior perpetuates and becomes excessive as we mature into adulthood, the extended pursuit of pleasure, in turn, results in stagnated growth, discomfort and, ultimately, *pain.*

Funny.

Ironically, it is the pursuit of challenge and its often-related incidental pain that yields our necessary personal growth, as well as a sense of accomplishment and, ultimately, pleasure. Both pleasure and pain are like "two sides of the same coin," or yin and yang (where the small dots signify the birth of its opposing force). You can pick your metaphor; there are plenty!

Recall that energy within a contained *environment* is never created or destroyed, but merely *transformed* (the first law of thermodynamics). So if I have a long balloon (air in a closed environment) – the type clowns might use to create balloon animals – and I squeeze one end of the balloon, where will the air pressure go?

In a contained environment the air pressure just moves to the other side of the balloon, but squeeze it too tight and it will pop!

If the balloon doesn't pop, the air pressure becomes greater on the opposite side – it becomes *imbalanced.*

Let's take another trip down memory lane, this time to our 8th grade science class. Do you happen to recall the scientific definition of *equilibrium?*

Equilibrium is the equal offset of pressures.

Interesting. "The equal offset of pressures."

Therefore, to attain a state of equilibrium both within the realm of science/physics *and* our human condition ("a state of intellectual and emotional poise"), it's apparent that pressure is *required.* It's even more apparent that the perpetual avoidance of pressure does not produce equilibrium, but (technically) its opposite: imbalance and distress.

There are essentially three possible responses when it comes to offsetting the pressure we feel in our lives:

1) To release it at the source. To depressurize; for instance, in the case of having physical pressures built up in the shoulders and back, a massage may be a way to release and reduce the pressure/tension.

2) To address it (prepare for it). To Plan, Prepare and Practice when and where applicable.

3) To avoid and/or ignore it (either unintentionally or intentionally). This is not always possible; it's usually a temporary solution involving procrastination, and it is rarely the best alternative.

For purposes of illustration, it's good to imagine three containers during an "equilibrium event" (though technically there is just one).

The first container is the *source* of the pressure that infiltrates a person's "space" or energy, affecting their existing state. It's typically an environmental (outside) component. It could be another person, a deadline for a project, an upcoming test, a business competitor, financial obligations, a friend or in-law, or perhaps even a sales target (such as a quarterly sales quota to be achieved).

The second container houses our *response*. When it comes to responding to pressure, it's important to recall the physics formula for pressure reviewed previously:

$$\text{Pressure} = \text{Force}/\text{Area}$$

We (humans) address and manipulate the right side of the equation (force or area) in order to alter the left side, which is the resultant pressure, to achieve equilibrium.

While this idea is mostly self-explanatory, it's probably worth noting that ancient Chinese medicine's holistic practices of acupuncture and acupressure are based upon the idea of releasing and freeing up energy blocks in order to improve energy flow. Illness, it is believed, is almost always the result of an obstruction to the natural healthy flow of "chi" – energy.

When we *respond* to pressure by planning, preparing and practicing, we effectively increase (strengthen and fortify) the *area* (our area, metaphorically), which in turn diminishes the force and the resultant pressure. The aim is to *equally offset the pressure.*

Finally, in many instances it is possible to **ignore** the pressure – either to put it off indefinitely or, more often than not, just delay it *temporarily* (procrastinate). Comedian Jon Stewart recently featured an urban dictionary term on his Comedy Central show called "procrasturbation." It's a funny word as it relates to pressure, since it would seem to serve multiple purposes.

To intentionally ignore and avoid pressure might be a recommended strategy when the pressure is identified as fabricated and unwarranted. Rather than coming from a real source – project, performance, deadline – it could be manufactured. An example of this might be a person who is overly concerned about what other people think about them (hyper-self-aware). Dwelling upon such a thought for too long creates undue distress and imagined pressures.

In instances like this, it's imperative to revisit Marcus Aurelius' challenge from the very beginning of this book: **"...to look things in the face and know them for what they are."**

There is a funny Bob Newhart sketch from MadTV (about five minutes) where the comedian (acting as a psychologist) counsels a young lady about her fabricated concerns, in this case, "being buried alive in a box." He assures her that their counseling session isn't likely to last more than four or five minutes, and, "I charge $5 for the first five minutes and then absolutely nothing after that." She replies, "It's almost too good to be true." Bob then asks

her, "Has anyone ever tried to bury you alive in a box?"
"No," she replies. Then, he commands her to, "*Stop it!*"
She becomes confused and a little angry. "But I can't," she
stammers. "It's been with me since childhood." Then, Bob
insists, "No. We don't go there." [aa]

When it comes to dealing with fabricated, emotional
and self-induced distress, "Just stop it!" is a perfect slogan
we can all incorporate in order to stop generating
unwarranted stress in our lives. Of course this technique is
possible only when we are willing to pay attention – to be
aware of our thoughts and our emotions.

[aa] https://www.youtube.com/watch?v=Ow0lr63y4Mw

Imbalance: Pressure is established. Container "A" is nearly full to the top – PRESSURE.

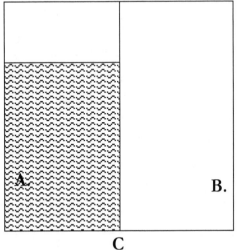

C
"C" equals the full container.

**EQUILIBRIUM is established –
equally offsetting the pressure in container "B"**

C

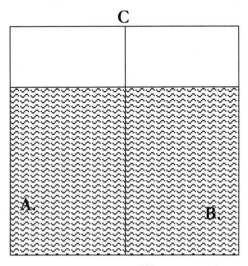

Last Father's Day I received a gag gift from my youngest daughter, Eva: a "Big Bucket of Silence." Picture a one-gallon bucket with the word SILENCE written, colored and taped to the front. Within the bucket were about 20 or so smaller pieces of paper with "silence" written on them, cut out as coupons or vouchers I could redeem with my daughters. I thought it was cute and fairly comical, and I'd forgotten that it was something I'd actually requested when they asked what I might want for Father's Day. My answer was in reference to our TV being on too loud and far too often.

However, that "gift" had me thinking a great deal about silence, particularly as it relates to pressure. "What," I wondered, as I reflected upon the **P=F/A** (Pressure=Force/Area) formula, "is the area of silence?" A bizarre question, I readily admit, but one that became extremely fascinating. I'd heard long ago that Einstein enjoyed engaging in such "thought experiments." He cites a famous one in his autobiography, suggesting it led to his theory of relativity: Envisioning himself riding a beam of light[51].

While this is certainly not relativity, or perhaps even physics, I found it to be a curious thought experiment: What *is* the area of silence? And what would happen if a great force met/collided with silence?

The idea was so captivating that I took to Google for further research, but the search engine produced just one obscure physics reference, essentially revealing nothing to answer the query, "What is the area of silence?" The empty result led me to believe I was onto something worthwhile, since the last time Google came up blank after one of my strange queries ("Why do habits exist?"), it led at least in part to me writing The Habit Factor[bb].

"What is the Area of Silence?" I kept wondering, speculating, even asking people (I suspect they thought I'd lost my marbles). While I continued to concentrate on this idea of silence (in silence), it turned out the only reasonable answer I could summon was that the Area of Silence was either 0 or ∞.

The fact that the "pure logic" of math was unable to compute either solution (dividing by 0 or ∞) just made me more curious.

As I imagined even the greatest force confronting (being divided by) silence, I thought: How could silence *ultimately* not win? I recalled a quote from long ago as I contemplated silence: "Everything emanates from silence and everything returns to silence. We are infinite."

The idea of Silence vs. Force reminded me of those superhero wars you envision as a child. For instance, what happens if Aquaman fights Spider-Man, Batman fights Superman, Incredible Hulk fights The Flash, etc.? But instead I envisioned comparing and contrasting supernatural (real) universal forces.

If the area of silence is 0, then *poof!* The force *ultimately* disappears. Similarly, even the greatest force, if divided by infinity – *poof!* It ultimately vanishes as well!

[bb] http://www.thehabitfactor.com/2012/11/beyond-the-power-of-habit-the-habit-factor-how-to-break-bad-habits-build-good-habits-part-one-get-unstuck-and-more/

Pressure, it turns out, has little chance against silence in the long run.

While the logic of math produces an "indeterminate" form,"[52] intuition suggests otherwise: Silence is more powerful than any force and, I think we can safely conclude, ultimately defeats any pressure.

You may think this type of thought experiment is nonsense, but it's worth reiterating what famed French mathematician, physicist and inventor Blaise Pascal once remarked of both logic and reason:

"The last function of reason is to recognize that there are an infinity of things which surpass it."

While the area of silence may be up for debate, what is not up for debate is the *value* of silence. Consider the ancient proverb "silence is golden." There is also a classic German proverb that says, "Silence is the fence around wisdom." Perhaps my favorite reference to silence comes from the ancient Chinese philosopher Lao Tzu: **"Silence is the source of great strength."**

I wanted to test this idea further, so I considered some historical greats who were not only subjected to immense pressure, but who also were incarcerated, for instance Mahatma Gandhi, Martin Luther King and Nelson Mandela.

I found myself discussing this concept with a friend, and he responded enthusiastically, "That's interesting; we just learned about St. Paul the Apostle and his writings of the *four prison epistles!*"

At the peak of each of their respective dramas, MLK, Nelson Mandela and Gandhi each were subjected to extended periods of solitude and silence.

This raises some key questions: Did silence play a major role in their lives? How were they refracting the pressures to which they were subjected? Could silence have contributed to their insight or equanimity? What are the chances that the solitude and silence of incarceration assisted in diffusing and offsetting the punishing pressures of being imprisoned? Taken further, did silence facilitate the achievement of their goals and intentions?

It's fairly well known that Mahatma Gandhi practiced the act of complete silence and would not speak for a period of 24 hours once a week. While under house arrest in 1943, Gandhi wrote a letter that has been described as "the most significant" in Indian history.[53]

On April 16, 1963, Martin Luther King, Jr. wrote his now famous "Letter from a Birmingham Jail." [54] In the letter he defends the strategy of nonviolent resistance to racism. His letter was a response to being referred to as an "outsider," and his rebuttal was that, "Injustice anywhere is a threat to justice everywhere." Further, his letter proved to be a vital position paper for the civil rights movement of the early 1960s.

In 1975, Nelson Mandela wrote the following while imprisoned:

"You may find that the cell is an ideal place to learn to know yourself, to search realistically and regularly the processes of your own mind and feelings. In judging our progress as individuals we tend to

concentrate on external factors such as one's social position, influence and popularity, wealth and standard of education .... but internal factors may be even more crucial in assessing one's development as a human being: honesty, sincerity, simplicity, humility, purity, generosity, absence of vanity, readiness to serve your fellow men – qualities within the reach of every soul – are the foundation of one's spiritual life .... at least, if for nothing else, the cell gives you the opportunity to look daily into your entire conduct to overcome the bad and develop whatever is good in you. Regular meditation, say of about 15 minutes a day before you turn in, can be fruitful in this regard. You may find it difficult at first to pinpoint the negative factors in your life, but the tenth attempt may reap rich rewards. Never forget that a saint is a sinner that keeps on trying." (Letter to Winnie Mandela from Kroonstad Prison, 1975)[55]

Do we need to be imprisoned to better manage our pressure and become a powerful leader or rally a great cause? Unlikely. However, these examples do affirm in an inverse – and perhaps perverse – way another powerful observation by the great Blaise Pascal:

"All men's miseries derive from not being able to sit in a quiet room alone."[*]

LANE THREE & AWARENESS

"Take away paradox from the thinker
and you have a professor."
~Soren Kierkegaard

A fairly famous author and speaker once told me that he didn't believe in habit. His intent was to underscore that he believed only in mindfulness (*all the time*). To be sure, such an objective is not just unsustainable, it's impossible, hence the existence of this beautiful and wonderful mechanism we call habit. Habit is a faculty so ingenious that it makes our behaviors easier and more efficient over time, while taxing our mental and physical energies less.

When a "guru" (which happens to be a four-letter word) tells you to walk a hard line – to follow one belief system or another – they have become, in essence, what Kierkegaard was warning against, what he felt professors symbolized: entities linear, dichotomous and black-and-white in their thinking.

While I'm a big fan of professors, I think Kierkegaard's point is an excellent one. When we become stuck on labels or single-mindedly focus upon any one way of thinking, we lose our ability to adapt and be flexible – to see the *whole* picture.

When there is just *one* right way judgments are created and, coincidentally, so are limitations. A great Zen saying emphasizes this point: "To the beginner the possibilities are limitless and to the expert, they are few."

Who learns a new subject more quickly? Someone with a Ph.D. or a 5-year-old? The child is totally open, nonjudgmental, a metaphorical sponge soaking up everything and rejecting nothing. He or she has no labels or filters, which only create friction and demand energy, slowing down the learning process.

I used to teach and train both adults and kids on how to use computers, and it would take the adults several times longer on average to learn the required skills and knowledge that the kids would learn almost instantly. My father, academically "gifted" as a young man, has never programmed and knows little if anything about software design, yet he continues to complain about "the idiots" who designed this software program or that one. Do his struggles become more or less difficult when he's fixated on how he believes the program *should* work as opposed to working within the existing parameters?

In working with various entrepreneur groups, it's not uncommon to notice a similar theme emerge: a fixation on a single strategy or idea, one answer – *the* answer!

So, depending on the latest trending business book or popular speaker, entrepreneurs readily will jump from one "paradigm shifting" idea to the next: "work smarter and not harder," or, "you gotta think outside the box." While these are wonderful clichés, they foster dichotomous (black-and-white) thinking.

One speaker advised our entrepreneur group, "You must always know what the customer wants!" Everyone nodded their heads in agreement; this was THE answer!

A month or so later a different speaker commanded, "Expectations! It's your expectations that will always equal your outcome." Everyone nodded their heads. These are the gems we've been looking for!

Shortly thereafter, we heard from another successful entrepreneur who shared why he thought his marriage was so strong and successful – why he and his wife were so happy. His secret: "Realizing I never have to settle!" I was so impressed by his conviction I recall writing that down and then circling it. "Never settle!"

Today, he's divorced.

Once again, life serves up a very special paradox. We think it is right to have goals and ideals and strive for them (and I believe it is); however, at the same time it is paramount that we remain flexible in our approach, ever-adapting and even unattached at times to any particular outcome. A good example of why retaining an open mind and flexible approach might be when 3M scientist Dr. Spencer Silver attempted to create a super-strong adhesive and inadvertently produced just the opposite – a pressure-sensitive, reusable, "low-tack" adhesive. Behold the Post-it Note!

What's become even more evident is that the more we fix our agenda, the more likely we are to encounter pressure and friction, sometimes positive and, unfortunately, sometimes negative.

So, for instance, the idea that "you must first know what the customer wants" sounds ingenious. However, Henry Ford once commented, "If I had asked people what they wanted, they would have said faster horses." Further, Steve Jobs – who referenced Ford's quote often, would say, "Customers don't know what they want until we've shown it to them," referencing devices such as the iPad and iPod.

My experience thus far has taught me to ask a different question any time I hear some terrific new strategy, business cliché or paradigm-shifting idea: "Could it be both?"

Could it be both?
- That we should work harder AND smarter?
- That we should think outside the box AND inside the box too?
- That we should have high expectations AND sometimes no expectations?
- That we need to know what the customer wants AND sometimes we must move with our gut and instinct?
- That we need to think long term AND short term?
- That there are no accidents AND there are indeed accidents?
- That we need to move quickly AND slowly?
- That we shouldn't settle AND sometimes maybe we should settle?
- That we should pay attention to the little things AND the big things?

- That we need passion AND/OR sometimes just an opportunity to be a successful entrepreneur[cc]?
- That it's the journey AND the destination?
- That the world is very big AND it is small?
- That you should think AND sometimes you should not think?
- That you should remain relaxed AND be on your toes?
- That pressure can be good AND bad?

Your turn:

- _____ AND _____

If I told you that you were absolutely, positively unique and special, would you agree? I hope so. You are. Now, doesn't that uniqueness make you just like everyone else? Since everyone is unique?

Therefore (*yes*), the answer is <u>BOTH</u>.

You are totally, positively unique AND you are just like everyone else.

Paradox, when fully grasped, serves our peace of mind since it removes friction. In effect, paradox aids the larger objective of understanding and accepting things as they are (and here's another great paradox) without necessarily understanding them!

[cc] Watch this video about passion vs. opportunity when you have time. It's by Entrepreneur.com, featuring Mike Rowe (around minute 10:00, http://www.entrepreneur.com/video/244959).

Paradox is not meant to be solved – just appreciated. Problems are meant to be solved, but nobody solves a real paradox.

Lao Tzu once allegedly wrote, "The words of truth are always paradoxical."

I suspect if he truly wrote that, or if it were translated correctly, it would read more like this: "The words of truth are *most often* paradoxical.

Eliminating the absolutes allows for flexibility, adaptability and understanding that perhaps we don't necessarily know everything. "I am the wisest man alive, for I know but one thing," Socrates once said. "That I know nothing."

It turns out that models and strategies can be wonderful and helpful tools, but as Heraclitus observed around 100 A.D., "You cannot step twice into the same river." So, no matter how well I might follow the model of your success, there is a good chance the location, timing or economy are different, while relationships and personalities are likely to be different, as well. That is not to say the strategy of modelling doesn't work; it often does. The caution is not to become entirely tied to one solution, particularly if the feedback indicates things aren't working.

In a very animated lunch interview with a former Navy SEAL, I ended up getting far more than I'd bargained for. I was just hoping to hear about his experience becoming a SEAL and the various pressure-related experiences. The ex-SEAL fit the prototypical SEAL personality – tough, humble, and I suspect mostly quiet, but not on this day. "That's the third lane, man!" JD kept repeating.

Perhaps it was because his girlfriend was in tow, or maybe that we'd had a couple of cocktails, or both, but the lunch extended into a second hour. "YOU are here!" He began to psychoanalyze my 35th birthday/existential crisis that resulted in me signing up for the Catalina Classic (a 32-mile open-ocean paddling event) about 10 years earlier.

He continued, "Your life had stagnated; you know, you believe you had something to offer, something else to do, something to give." He continued, "But your 'entrepreneur/tech guy, family guy' things are 'cushy.' He used air quotes and then continued, ". . . and things are comfortable and you're feeling like something is missing, *right?*" He's working hard to convince me of something, so I just nod my head and agree, "Sure."

"Well guess what, man?" he continued. "It's like this!" He pulled out a napkin and drew three parallel lines, representing a few "lanes." "You are here! Let's call it Lane 1, and here is everyone else, let's call that Lane 2!" (I never asked him why I wasn't in the same lane with everyone else. But I suspected that was beside the point, and now I know it was.) Then he drew an "X" on the outside. "THIS!" He pounded the pen hard on the napkin and then circled it…"This is it man! This is the third lane!"

Pointing to me, he said, "You! You had to go and get out here – to jump into Lane 3 to challenge yourself, to show you are different, to let everyone know you are the man!" He's almost screaming at this point, very intense, and his girlfriend is just nodding her head.

I smiled at her, chuckle a little, and started to think maybe he's nuts. He continued talking, but his words began to fade. The more I let his earlier statement sink in, the more I began to think he might be onto something. His voice got my attention again. "Think about it! That paddling event of yours, that doesn't even exist in those first two lanes, does it?"

"Nope," I agree, shaking my head once again.

Then, he began to tell his own personal story. "Look, I was either going to jail or going to die. My friends weren't into much good, so I needed a third lane, get it?

"So, I F'n enlisted!

"I knew that I needed to become a Navy SEAL!"

It's now nearly a year after our engaging conversation, and I see how the pieces fit. JD drew a perfect analogy – a beautiful parallel, really (both figuratively and literally) relating to our obligation to check up, to examine our life, to identify and ask ourselves, "How are things going, *really*?"

What's interesting is that the Entrepreneur.com video referenced just a few pages earlier has Mike Rowe saying, "They [entrepreneurs] got to a point in their lives where they realized they had to make money. So they looked around at where everyone else was going and *they just went the other way*."

JD said it one way, Mike Rowe said it another, and of course Socrates put it this way: "The unexamined life is not worth living."

In essence, they are all saying the same thing: "Where's the third lane?"

The third lane is the result of the examined life. Chances are good that if you even ask yourself the question, "Where's my third lane?" you'll get an immediate answer.

The third lane requires your personal experience plus your reflection.

Lane 1: Where you are now.

Lane 2: Where everyone else is.

Lane 3: Where do you want to go?

The third lane often involves a new setting or environment and, of course, a new challenge. It's where there is opportunity and – you got it – a whole lot of pressure.

The third lane is the change lane and the passing lane. It's the lane that's most uncomfortable and is likely to test you every step of the way. And that's how you know you're in the right lane!

When Eleanor Roosevelt declared, "You must do the things you think you cannot do," she was directing you to the third lane. All creativity resides in the third lane. And here's what else we know about the third lane: It requires humility, reflection and *courage*. The courage to accept yourself and present conditions, the courage to test yourself and fail, and the humility that self-reflection required of you to make the shift.

Another key to the third lane is what personal development legend Jim Rohn declared decades ago: **The true value of a goal is not in the goal itself, but in the person you have to become to achieve it.**

Think about that. That's the power of the third lane, the power of goal-setting. The third lane forces you to <u>plan,</u> <u>prepare</u> and <u>practice,</u> and in return you must grow stronger. Metaphorically, your *area* increases due to the increased force of the challenge, and by responding to the challenge

appropriately you become stronger, more content and
balanced.

You may be wondering, Do I want equilibrium (balance,
peace and harmony), or do I want the third lane?

And I suspect you know the answer by now

It's both!"

Take a good look at these two lines below.

Which might be more alive?

Which is more peaceful, at rest (although if you consider
it further, perhaps it's not "dead"?

Hence the significance of **awareness** – that is, knowing
when and in which direction to *adjust* can be a result only of
the examined life.

Recall Einstein's brilliant statement about balance and
you gain even more insight into the enigmatic concept: that
balance (as it's sought in human existence) is more a *result*,
than any particular moment in time.

Balance, as we know it might just simply be action plus
awareness plus more action (in the form of adjustments).

"Life is like riding a bicycle." Einstein was quick to point out, "You need to keep moving to stay balanced."

Are you moving AND adjusting?

Action + Awareness + Adjustment = Balance

Ideally there is even awareness prior to the first action.

So, if I took a picture of a tight-rope walker (a quick snapshot), she would most likely appear off balance (at a particular moment caught on camera). Yet, when she makes it to the other side of the rope, she artistically reveals the *resultant* balance.

Throughout our lives we've noticed a perpetual, organic dance within nature and even within our own biology. Rhythmically we have our own self-adjusting and natural (circadian) rhythms – even our blood PH is in a constant quest to find balance. In nature, we notice high tides and low tides, low-pressure weather patterns followed by high-pressure weather, and on and on – the *cycle* continues – all in order to create a *resultant balance.*

Dan Millman, author of *The Way of the Peaceful Warrior,* recently described what he called his favorite definition of enlightenment: "A state of mind and body where you alternate from the heights of ecstasy to the depths of despair, all at the speed of light."[56]

While I'm not sure if that would be my definition, it fits nicely here, since at the speed of light the *resultant* state could only be one of total equanimity, created of course via lively, ambitious and self-correcting oscillation.

MASTERY

> *"The Master never reaches for the great;*
> *thus she achieves greatness. When she runs into*
> *a difficulty, she stops and gives herself to it.*
> *She doesn't cling to her own comfort;*
> *thus problems are no problem for her."*
> ~Lao Tzu, Tao Te Ching

Like many college graduates I spent nearly a full summer backpacking throughout Europe. In Amsterdam, I met a beautiful young lady who invited me to visit her back home in California. I lived on the coast and she lived far inland. On what you might consider a "date," I learned she'd had a baby (surprise!), a beautiful little boy about eight months old. Now, that should have been the most memorable detail of the evening, but it was topped by a comment she made a bit later, something I haven't been able to shake. We were talking about surfing and she said, "Yeah, my dad used to surf but he *mastered* it."

Even back then I sensed something was amiss with her statement. Now, some 25 years later, it's clear. True mastery, in perfect paradoxical fashion, is never attained; that is, the master who believes he has arrived hasn't, and the master who knows he'll never arrive, has (or *will* or *can*).

Nobody "masters" surfing and, as you might guess, nobody "masters" life. Certainly there are people who excel in many pursuits. And while they don't give out trophies for life "mastery," they do give out championship trophies in professional surfing and most other sports.

Incredibly, the essence of true mastery just might lie within, of all things, a brilliant Tweet shared by 11-time World Professional Surfing Champion Kelly Slater: **"Every day is day one."**

Whether you're a fan of surfing or not, chances are you can appreciate "greatness," and what Kelly Slater has managed to do is hard, if not impossible, to parallel in any other individual or team sport. The man has book-ended his professional career with championships, meaning he's been both the *youngest* and *oldest* pro surfer to finish the pro tour in first place.

While the word "legend" gets thrown around a lot these days, Robert Kelly Slater fits the bill perfectly. Lance Armstrong once tweeted of Kelly that he "may be the best athlete of all time." (This was well before Lance's PED scandal.)

Kelly has so dominated professional surfing that over a 20-year-plus span, he's won an incredible and unprecedented 11 world titles, and in the years that he didn't win, he finished in the top five nearly every time. To try to put 11 titles into perspective, the former surf champion with the most titles was Mark Richards, who won four in the 1980s. Kelly has nearly tripled that previous title record.

It's worth adding that today's high-performance surfing requires even greater athleticism than in years past, and a large majority of the maneuvers (particularly aerials – tricks above the wave/out of the water) didn't even exist when Slater first joined the tour. Today, Kelly's doing maneuvers that weren't even conceivable when he turned pro. In fact, at 42 (yes, 42) years old, he performed an aerial that took the surf community by surprise and was then reported by seemingly every mainstream media outlet, including Huffington Post, TMZ, Fox Sports and ESPN [1] (watch the video below!).

Even more remarkable is that Kelly is competing against "kids" half his age now (in a sport that favors youth) and does so oftentimes in dangerous and even deadly surf – and he just keeps *winning*. The "average" pro surfer tends to stop competing in his early 30s, if he makes it that long, and by then he's already considered "old." Kelly's consistency of peak performance over two decades is out of this world. Sometimes I think he may be an alien.

While I don't know Kelly personally, I'm willing to bet that he plans, prepares and practices more and better than any pro surfer *ever*. And when you couple that with a mastery mindset – *"every day is day one"* – you have a perfect recipe for mastery.

Now, for purposes of our analysis, it may be fitting that the medium in which Kelly displays his unique mastery is within one of life's most precious elements – water. And, it turns out that the further one distills (no pun intended) the essential principles of mastery, the more they appear to nicely overlap with the remarkable qualities of *water*.

---

[1] http://espn.go.com/video/clip?id=11718370

So, for instance, is an aspiring master adaptable or fixed? Is she accepting and soft or rejecting and hard?

How about water?

It's no secret that our bodies are more than 60 percent water, our brain and muscles are more than 75 percent water, and our blood is approximately 92 percent water. Now consider that the earth is covered by approximately 71 percent water, and I suspect we might all be able to learn a little something about "mastering" life by harmonizing ourselves with its very essence – good ol' H2O!

Here are just *some* of the core qualities of water we might consider.

Water is:

1) Adaptive: Flexible and formless
2) Patient: It is in no hurry; it might rush forth like a wave or stay quiet and still like a lake
3) Resilient: Never gives up and will even change form if necessary
4) Self-balancing/correcting: Adjusts to pressure/environmental influence and always finds equanimity – perfect PH balance
5) Strong: It's strength on a molecular level and supernatural level is legendary
6) Smooth and soft: Water has no harsh edges
7) Transparent: There is no subterfuge; its clarity allows us to see into its depths
8) Deliberate: No confusion of its intentions; it knows where it wants to go
9) Consistent: Water always behaves in the same manner and has the same nature

10) Cohesive: Allows for the development of surface
tension, the capacity to withstand tension and stress
11) Solvent: Simply known within science as the
  universal solvent. Scientifically, *water is considered the
  ultimate solution*

How well do you match up with these qualities? Are you
cohesive (team building), consistent, transparent, and
smooth (non-abrasive in your relationships)? To that end,
I'm reminded of Thomas Jefferson's sage advice when it
came to interpersonal skills: "Always take things by their
smooth handle." Further, are you self-balancing, self-
correcting (recall the third lane), flexible, patient, adaptive
and solvent? (Think financial.)

So while the simple message could just be "drink more
water," the essence of the message is really that *both peace of
mind and mastery (not coincidently) share many of the pronounced
characteristics of water.*

To underscore that observation, Robert Greene, author
of *Mastery*, explains a wonderful concept about how creative
masters, for example Einstein or Mozart, were able to
exhibit something he's identified as *fluidity* (an interesting
term given our discussion of Mastery and Water above): A
truly creative master can hold two diametrically opposed
viewpoints (embracing paradox), and balance them (weave
in and out) to create a third alternative or solution.

He likens this sort of creativity to that of a child
combined with the knowledge attained by an adult, a
specialist in a subject matter. Greene shares a term coined

by famous psychiatrist Carl Jung, who made a similar observation and called it "serious play."

I'm reminded of a classic tale told by Norman Vincent Peale, shared long ago, about a large truck (think 18-wheeler) stuck under a bridge. When a father and son came upon the accident, they saw scores of police and firefighters trying hard to pull the truck free. The truck was wedged so tight it seemed impossible; they were all at a standstill. All these men had spent hours trying to pull the truck free, to no avail. The little boy, however, saw the problem entirely differently. He turned to his father and asked, "Why don't they just let the air out of the tires?"

While it's advisable for the aspiring master to retain a child's mind for creativity, it's important to underscore that all acts of creativity demand courage. Therefore, the truly aspiring master will have to displace her own self-doubts and fears. She will need to press forward – into the unknown – to embrace uncertainty.

Will she be able to do it?

Well, when it comes to fear, Cus D'Amato, former trainer and mentor to ex-heavyweight champion professional boxer Mike Tyson, shared this idea with Mike and his other boxers: "The hero and the coward both feel the same thing, but the hero uses his fear, projects it onto his opponent, while the coward runs. *It's the same thing*, fear, but it's what you do with it that matters."

When Cus says *"it's what you do with it that matters,"* you can safely assume he's talking about refracting the pressure (fear) *positively*. And this is the essence of an aspiring master: realizing that only *you* retain the ability to refract *positively*, to redefine the influences and influencers in your life and perceive them as favorable.

"But," you may say, "what if they are not favorable?"

That is a fair question and maybe even an accurate observation; there is a very good chance that circumstances may *not* be favorable. However, the question remains: Which *response* will help to serve your goals and ideals, a positive one or a negative one?

In many ways we've come full circle: Mastery (and peace of mind) must be the result of energy well-used and a mind that's properly applied. This was touched upon earlier in a powerful quote by Brian Tracy: "High-achieving men and women are simply those who know how to use their minds better than low-achieving men and women."

This must be the residence of any aspiring master: the domain of the mind.

When it comes to the concept of positive thinking, people will sometimes roll their eyes and say things like, "Positive thinking…blah blah blah." In response, I like to refer to Zig Ziglar's classic rebuttal: "Positive thinking won't help you do everything, it'll just help you do everything better."

Do we need negativity? Absolutely! From a holistic standpoint, it's impossible *not* to have it. Just like a battery has a positive and negative charge, so too will our lives be influenced by negativity (mostly in the form of problems). In fact, you might regard all challenges and difficulties from a holistic standpoint simply as negatively charged situations. Therefore, it's imperative that we respond to each challenge positively!

If that still isn't convincing enough for you, it's important to consider that your very perception of things such as pressure and stress has been scientifically proven to influence your well-being, health and, I'm sure, peace of mind.

In her inspiring and informative 2013 TED talk, Kelly McGonigal, Ph.D., shared some of the latest research validating many of these ideas about pressure and stress (here easily interchanged). While she was referring specifically to stress and its toll on human health, recognize the value of applying these ideas to pressure.

Here is just a snippet of her TED talk. To see the entire presentation, please visit the link below.

How to Make Stress Your Friend, TEDGlobal 2013][dd] [Excerpt: Kelly McGonigal]

>> 0:39

> … My confession is this: I am a health psychologist, and <u>my mission is to help people be happier and healthier.</u> But I fear that something I've been teaching for the last 10 years is doing more harm than good, and it has to do with stress. For years I've been telling people, stress makes you sick. It increases the risk of everything from the common cold to cardiovascular disease. *Basically, I've turned stress into the enemy.* But I have changed my mind about stress, and today, I want to change yours.

[dd]http://www.ted.com/talks/kelly_mcgonigal_how_to_make_stress_your_friend

>>1:20

Let me start with the study that made me rethink my whole approach to stress. This study tracked 30,000 adults in the United States for eight years, and they started by asking people, "How much stress have you experienced in the last year?" They also asked, "Do you believe that stress is harmful for your health?" And then they used public death records to find out who died.

>>1:47

(Laughter)

>>1:48

Okay. Some bad news first. People who experienced a lot of stress in the previous year had a 43 percent increased risk of dying. But that was only true for the people who also believed that stress is harmful for your health. (Laughter) People who experienced a lot of stress but did not view stress as harmful were no more likely to die. In fact, they had the lowest risk of dying of anyone in the study, including people who had relatively little stress.

>>2:23

Now the researchers estimated that over the eight years they were tracking deaths, 182,000 Americans died prematurely, not from stress, but from the belief that stress is bad for you. (Laughter) That is over 20,000 deaths a year. Now, if that estimate is correct, that would make believing stress is bad for you the 15th largest cause of death in the United States last year, killing more people than skin cancer, HIV/AIDS and homicide.

>>2:55

(Laughter)

>>2:58

You can see why this study freaked me out. Here I've been spending so much energy telling people stress is bad for your health.

>>3:07

So this study got me wondering: *Can changing how you think about stress make you healthier?* And here the science says **YES!**. When you change your mind about stress you can change your body's response to stress.

[Bolding and underlining added for emphasis.]

So, here's scientific evidence confirming the very precepts that we've outlined from the beginning: how pressure and its variants – stress, anxiety, challenge, and setbacks – are perceived, as valuable or harmful, not only influences a situation's outcome, but can dramatically change the present moment and thereby our well-being and peace of mind.

Not only does the aspiring master retain the ability to reframe information and perceptions – to use the mind constructively to help guide a desired outcome – she has the unique ability to creatively connect the dots, to view problems *opportunistically*. In our golf group, we have a great saying after a player hits a bad shot; typically someone will shout out, "That's another opportunity for greatness!"

There happens to be a great Zen koan about two monks who are arguing about a flag as it flaps in the wind.

"It's the wind that is moving!" says the first monk. "No! It is the flag that is moving!" says the second monk adamantly. Just then, a Zen master walks by and overhears

the argument. He calmly states, "You are both incorrect...
it is your *mind* that is moving."

Your mind is always moving, even at rest. Becoming
aware of the mind – respecting its power and at the same
time knowing how to balance elements that are within your
control and those that are outside your circle of influence –
will greatly contribute to your peace of mind.

When it comes to peace of mind there is a famous
prayer entitled, of all things, *The Serenity Prayer*, and it's been
adopted by Alcoholics Anonymous. The prayer was
authored by American theologian Reinhold Niebuhr and it
goes like this:

**God, grant me the serenity to accept the things I
cannot change,
The courage to change the things I can,
And the wisdom to know the difference.**

Finally, to emphasize this idea further, there is a
wonderful ancient Chinese parable about a farmer It's a
terrific reminder that while we are in control of certain
things, it can be futile to fight and attempt to control things
over which we have no influence. In fact, the story even
reminds us of the importance of surrendering and
embracing uncertainty.

The story goes like this:

Once upon a time there was a Chinese farmer who lost a horse; it ran away. All the neighbors came around later that same evening and shared their concern, saying, "Oh my, we're so sorry," and "That's just too bad."

The wise farmer replied, "Maybe."

The very next day the horse returned and it brought seven wild horses back to the farm with it.

Later that evening all the neighbors once again gathered around and they reveled in his good fortune. "Wow!" they exclaimed. "That's terrific news; you are so lucky!"

To which the wise farmer replied, "Maybe."

The next day the farmer's son was attempting to break in one of the wild horses. As he was riding the horse it threw him to the ground and broke his leg badly.

Later that evening, the neighbors visited to console the farmer and to see how the son was doing. They expressed their concern and regret, saying, "Well, that is so unfortunate, isn't it?"

To which the wise farmer replied, "Maybe."

The very next day officers from the Chinese army came knocking on the farmer's door intent on drafting his son for a recent war that had started. However, they quickly noticed that he had a broken leg and would be of no use to them.

As you might expect, later that evening all the neighbors came around and said, "Wow! Isn't that wonderful luck you have, your son doesn't have to go to war!"

To which the wise farmer replied, "Maybe."

REVIEW: PEACE OF MIND
QUESTIONS AND ACTIONS

- What keeps *you* up at night?
- Is the pressure in your life being channeled toward a positive, hopeful outcome – or a negative one?
- How can you apply imagination to problem-solving and real-life ordeals and solutions?
- How can embracing the circumstances we cannot control, rather than fighting them, make things easier?
- What does an accepting mindset bring along with it?
- What are some ways you can offset the pressures of your current situation, helping you to retain equilibrium?
- How does having a purpose serve to refract enormous pressure?
- What is "grit," and how does this quality help one achieve goals in the face of pressure?
- No pressure, no grit! Where can you find a place without pressure and problems?
- Why would the constant pursuit of pleasure ultimately lead to stagnancy and pain?
- How does the perpetual avoidance of pressure create not equilibrium, but (technically) its opposite: imbalance and distress?
- How can we increase (strengthen and fortify) our *area* (metaphorically) to diminish the force of current pressures?
- Are you creating emotional and self-induced distress?

- What two words can you tell yourself to prevent such self-induced stress?
- What is the "area" of silence?
- How does silence contribute to insight and equanimity?
- How can you use silence as a tool to refract pressure?
- How does accepting paradox figure into a success mindset?
- How can an open mind and a flexible approach yield greater success?
- What is the "third lane" – and how can you get there?
- What traits are needed to enter the "third lane"?
- How is balance, as we know it, really a *result* vs. a moment in time?
- What is mastery? Is it ever truly achieved?
- How does the mastery mindset imitate the qualities of water?
- How do the hero and the coward differ in the face of pressure and fear?
- Where does the aspiring master "reside"?
- How can your perception of pressure/stress influence your well-being?
- How can embracing uncertainty bring serenity?
- Has something terrible happened that you are sure is terrible? Could it be a "maybe" situation?

Be sure to visit:
ThePressureParadox.com/prism **for your FREE**
Pressure P.R.I.S.M. Assessment!

Actions!

- ⏲ Practice "choosing" your response to the next problem/crisis that arises.
- ⏲ Find the "beauty" within your current chaos.
- ⏲ Pinpoint people you know, or know of, who demonstrate the ability to properly respond, adapt and evolve to deal with unimaginable pressures.
- ⏲ In the midst of a pressure-packed situation, reflect upon your *purpose* – use it as a tool to refract the current pressures.
- ⏲ Plan, Prepare and Practice for an upcoming event/responsibility/assignment and see how the process alleviates pressure.
- ⏲ Practice the idea of "Just Stop It" in an area of your life where you're creating self-induced distress.
- ⏲ Consciously use silence as a tool in a pressure-packed situation.
- ⏲ When presented with the latest wisdom, strategy or business cliché, practice asking, "Could it be *both*?"
- ⏲ Practice consciously eliminating the absolutes in your environment/mindset to allow for flexibility, adaptability and understanding – perhaps we may not have all the information.
- ⏲ Identify your own personal "third lane."
- ⏲ Think about the pronounced traits of water and how they reflect the mastery mindset; focus on nurturing these qualities in your character.

EPILOGUE

THE PSYCHOLOGY OF BECOMING

*"They both listened silently to the water, which
to them was not just water, but the voice of life,
the voice of Being, the voice of perpetual
Becoming." ~Hermann Hesse, Siddhartha*

At the age of four my daughter Mia loved to draw and
paint. At this young age she was fabulously artistic and
seemed to be tapped into an unrelenting force – a stream of
creativity.

One night driving home with our daughters in the car
we witnessed a magnificent sunset; upon arriving home, Mia
took out her pens and crayons and began drawing. When
we later asked what she was doing, she exclaimed that she
wanted to "create the sunset!"

Perhaps not an entirely unique experience for parents of
toddlers; however, a few days later, early on a Sunday
morning, something fairly mysterious took place.

I awoke to find her there again drawing at the table.
Only this time, she was writing. Some quick background:
Our dog Hercules, "Herc," had just passed away about two
months earlier, and we'd lost Mia's wonderful grandmother
not too long before that. Without getting too eccentric, it's
safe to say that their departure still didn't feel entirely real.

So, early that morning I came upon Mia's writing and my jaw dropped. I tried to process what I was looking at.

In fact, even today it's incomprehensible.

There, scribbled in her best four-year-old writing was our dog's name "Hrkles," but it was what she wrote above it that was so captivating.

"Metamorphisis = Die" (first line with an equals sign)

"Metamorphis is Die" (second line with word "is")

"HrKLes" (third line in box)

Granted, her spelling was off, but to me this wasn't about spelling. There was nothing nearby – no cartoons, no kids' books or magazines, nothing she could copy these words or ideas from. Thinking about it now, if she *had* copied the words they most likely would not have been misspelled.

I questioned her immediately. "What is this?" I asked, holding the artwork in front of her face. "Mia, what is this, why did you write this?" She was totally confused by my mild interrogation. I pressed further, "Do you know what this means...do you know what *metamorphosis* is?"

She was as baffled as you might expect any four-year-old to be. Not only did she not know the word, she had no idea why she wrote it or why I was asking so many questions.

I did my best to control myself; I didn't want to rattle her any more than I probably had or make her feel self-conscious. Before I could ask any more questions, she was off to play with her next toy.

I was frozen, staring at this piece of paper and wondering if I should even show it to my wife. Her mother's recent passing would undoubtedly raise some emotions. I took out my camera and snapped a couple of pictures of Mia's scribbles.

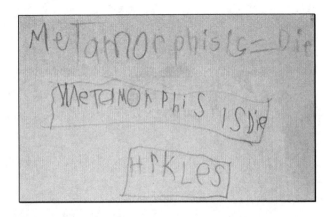

Now, over 10 years later, I think it's finally "safe" to share this story and photo. Of course, none of us have any more answers as to what transpired that day; my daughter, now almost 15, has little if any recollection.

At the time I suggested to my wife that this was the type of "event" that, if we did share with friends or family, would wind us up on the nightly news. Or, perhaps in one of those bizarre situations where people line up outside the door to see spiritual apparitions of a "Madonna," or Jesus on a piece of pizza or something.

Nothing we'd really want any part of.

So, why share this inexplicable story now?

Well, let's reconsider the message – a message that was scribbled and reaffirmed *twice*.

"Metamorphosis equals Die" "Metamorphosis is Die"

That's extremely powerful. However, perhaps even more powerful is the following awareness:

"Metamorphosis *equals* <u>*Living*</u>**"**
"Metamorphosis *is* <u>*now*</u>**"**

Do you recall what you looked like at five years old? How about how you viewed the world at five? Do you happen to recall your beliefs and understandings then? What about at 17 years old? How about now? How do they differ? Muhammad Ali once commented, "The man who views the world at 50 the same as he did at 20 has wasted 30 years of his life."

How do you think you'll physically look at 85 (assuming you're alive) and, perhaps more importantly, how do you think you'll view the world? (Stop and really think about that.) Do you think your beliefs will be the same as they are now? Is that easy to do or difficult to contemplate?

From a biological perspective, it's important to recognize every living cell in our body is being regenerated time and again – and this process continues over the course of our lives. Dr. Frisen, a stem cell biologist at the Karolinska Institute in Stockholm, believes that "the average age of <u>all</u> the cells in an adult's body may turn out to be as young as 7 to 10 years."[57]

From a physics perspective, I'm reminded of the first law of thermodynamics (reviewed earlier), the Law of Conservation, which affirms, "Energy cannot be created or destroyed; it can only be changed from one form to another." This is the law that fuels a constant metamorphosis – a perpetual becoming.

Therefore, *your transformation* is an imminent reality and it's worth the reminder that you are changing right now. Famous inventor, author and theorist Buckminster Fuller once noted, "There is nothing in a caterpillar that tells you it's going to be a butterfly."

Yet, have we become so fixated upon our current and past self – and even our past, troubled issues and results – to forget about the transformative forces in effect right now?

It's incredible to think that unlike any other creature on the planet we can uniquely guide and determine our future being/form and character. A cheetah isn't likely to become a hippo (not in this lifetime), nor will a whale turn into a monkey. Although fun to imagine.

We witness these remarkable transformations all around us: the 75-year-old man who becomes a body builder; the guy who completes the Ironman triathlon who only 18 months earlier was 200 pounds overweight; the five-year-old girl who morphs into a 26-year-old doctor or lawyer; the 12-year-old girl who becomes an Olympic gold medalist.

"When I let go of who I am, I become what I might be." Another Lao Tzu classic from ages ago.

So, you are encouraged not only to let go of the past, but perhaps your past identity as well, and to recognize and appreciate your unique capacity to *direct your transformation in any direction you'd like – right now.* There is no need to wait. In fact, it's happening anyway. And, isn't this yet another terrific paradox – that one of the great constants in life is change?

It's this awareness that really begets a new and important question, one that we all have an obligation to ask *and* answer:

"**Who** (not what) do I want to <u>Become</u>?"

Then, begin! Direct your *Becoming* – start your transformation *now*. Apply these forces (habit and pressure) in the very same manner that the greatest achievers throughout history already have. Use these supernatural gifts for what they were intended: your transformation (*your becoming*), to help you create your ideal future – your success!

21 Questions, Plus a Few Bonuses

*"Time is a great teacher; unfortunately
she kills all her pupils." ~Unknown*

1) **After one has achieved a certain level of success, how do you
    avoid drifting and remain committed to higher goals?**
    It seems that the "true greats" appear not to celebrate any
    one victory too long. They seek out new challenges right
    away. The Mastery Mindset (see "Mastery" chapter) dictates
    that every day is "day one," meaning new opportunities are
    ever-present, allowing you to learn, grow and become better.

2) **How can one balance pressure so you can enjoy high achievement
    of goals without stress?**
    Taking a cue from the "Lane Three" chapter, the idea is to be
    aware and notice being stressed; to oscillate – move
    between – achievement and pressure (positive and negative)
    when necessary. By analyzing our results, language and
    thoughts, we can quickly gauge our real stress levels. It's
    important to recall that balance ought to be viewed as a
    result (recall tightrope walker) and not a moment in time.

3) **Can you use the creation of habits to reduce pressure and at the
    same time use (channel) pressure to your advantage?**
    Few things are more *familiar* than habit (known as "second
    nature") and routine; paradoxically, that can sometimes work
    in our favor and sometimes work against us. Interestingly,

when it comes to reducing pressure, routine and habit are perfect for de-stressing. Consider the pro basketball player who will go through a routine (series of habits) before he shoots a high-pressure shot. He bounces the ball 10 times...then spins it in his hands...bounces it some more...bends his knees...etc. This helps to reduce pressure, or to be more accurate, keeps the player from thinking too much – becoming too self-aware. So, pressure can help to forge habits that can later reduce pressure when it comes to performance (via habituation).

4) **I have very high expectations of my team to perform to my standards, and when they don't, I get very upset. Am I putting unreasonable pressure on them and myself to expect them to care as much, think as much, and perform like I do?**

This is a wonderful and complex question. At the surface (assuming you are the owner of the business), it is unfair to expect your team to care as much as you do unless they are owners as well. Having said that, my experience is that the vast majority of employees want to feel worthwhile and believe they are *contributing*. So, I will revert to something I discussed with a manager recently. As the entrepreneur/owner, it's your responsibility to take ownership. Is there a way you can train and educate your team more often and better? Is there a way to communicate better priorities and values? Unfortunately, just saying "we've trained them" doesn't get you off the hook. Ownership of the business and the corresponding problems are yours, and that is the first step to correcting the problem.

5) Is there a danger to becoming "immune" to pressure when using it as a constant motivator? Can you build up a tolerance to it as a positive/motivational force?

> The idea is to build a healthy tolerance. Healthy is subjective, and everyone owns the responsibility for that awareness and understanding. Do you think a Navy SEAL has a higher tolerance for pressure situations than a star athlete? Who's to say what is too much or what is not enough? The best gauge tends to be the clues left by the results, which are always there to view and analyze. What's interesting to me is, as you move up the responsibility "food chain," you tend to notice a corresponding level of pressure. You can bet that the president of your company or organization has greater pressures than the intern. The president of the United States has greater pressure than the vice president, etc.

6) Much of the book focuses on how to use pressure to improve individual performance. A lot of what you recommend can be easily used at the team level, but I'm wondering if you have any additional tips for using pressure in the context of team collaboration.

> From my experience, a "team" can be as simple as two or three people, and those types of teams tend to be great for accountability to generate <u>positive peer pressure</u>. The best tip may be to ensure that both time and caution are invested in selecting the right people to participate; this can make all the difference. Are the members committed or interested? (See the "Comfort Kills" chapter.) 1) Select the "right," committed people; 2) Communicate openly and establish a rhythm – accountability calls every Tuesday at noon, for example. These can be as short as 5-15 minutes (even with 12 members). 3) Keep groups small (under eight) if possible.

7) **If pressure can be a good thing for performance, does an individual need to feel some level of pressure to reach peak performance?**

> Typically, the answer is yes. If you were to reverse-engineer some of the greatest "peak performances," I think you'd be hard-pressed to find outcomes that were without an "air of pressure." A peak performance suggests a better-than-average result. So, typically, to achieve a higher level of *focus*, pressure is a requirement – as is planning, preparing and practicing (the 3 P's).

8) **In a team setting, what happens when individuals on the team feel different levels of pressure to perform? Should the leader set the tone?**

> I think the short answer is yes. Typically leaders will set the tone, be it a manager or a quarterback or a safety on a football team. The players tend to feed off the "leader." A great example of this is former Ravens linebacker Ray Lewis; he was always sure to set the tone. And, ultimately, his team won an NFL championship and Lewis was the MVP. Typically, a *good* leader uses and shares the pressure felt in a positive way to encourage a great vision and belief about how the company or team _will_ respond that they can buy into.

9) **I love some of the examples you use about pressure as it relates to sports and athletes. How has your understanding of pressure changed the way that you watch sporting events? Do you find it easier to predict who will win a sporting event?**

> I'm not sure my prognostication skills have improved any, but since this is somewhat fresh, I haven't really viewed or made any predictions through such a lens. What I can tell you is that the best "bet," so to speak, is with the athlete or team who Plans, Prepares and Practices the best and most often.

There is a reason, for instance, in the NFL (and really, all pro leagues) that top assistant coaches are "poached" after they've won a championship. This is because it's believed these individuals know "the formula" for success (that is, what it takes in the form of <u>planning</u>, <u>preparing</u> and <u>practicing</u>). When it comes to individual players, the "winner" in the long run, more often than not is the one with the "Mastery" mindset, who believes that "every day is day one," the one who develops the habits of the 3 P's. "The Grinders." (See "No Pressure – No Diamonds" chapter.) For instance, Jason Day struggled for many years in PGA events – he even said he "choked back in 2011." Later, he appropriately recognized that, "Most of the time if you're a master of something, you failed more times than you've won." Recently, though, he's been on a tear, winning the PGA Championship and The Barclays and even more recently the BMW Championship. After the BMW Championship, he said this about pressure: "You're not thinking about mistakes; you're thinking about what could possibly happen (positive)...you wash it out of your head...(negative). There is no stress... obviously there is stress, but I'm enjoying it – it's *good pressure."*

10) **When I'm overwhelmed by the amount of projects (not the importance of the projects), how do I deal with performing under the pressure of overwhelm?**

Overwhelm is typically a feeling of stress, or distress – of being *stretched too thin*. This typically occurs when we have not taken the time to identify <u>one</u> priority. It's important to recognize that if you have 10 priorities you really have none, and correspondingly, that lack of focus leads to distress.

11) If I have a routine task that doesn't feel urgent or difficult, how can I use pressure to improve performance for mundane tasks?

Try to make a game out of it. One of the best gifts I've received in a long time is an inexpensive, 4-minute (old school) sand timer. To get started and stay focused to create some positive pressure, I just plop the 4-minute timer down and challenge myself to write for 4 minutes, or respond to e-mails, or whatever – for just 4 minutes! The key is that the fabricated pressure greatly facilitates *focus*. In this ADD world, it's a perfect tool to push through the mundane tasks. When you can gamify things even a little, you bring about the element of competition, which increases pressure. It's worth noting that this is what drives the Olympians and the great athletes – *the pressure of competition*. This competitive pressure often transcends sports; you see it in apps and games, and you might even say that the competitive pressure of the Cold War drove our scientists to produce and innovate faster than the competition. Creating mini-peer groups and having them compete in a *positive environment* is very effective.

12) I have been told that if I'm under "pressure" all day, that leads to burnout. Is that true?

Anything done all day will result in a form of burnout. If you slept all day, you'd be off balance. If you eat all day, you wouldn't feel right. Certainly, working all day will burn you out. This goes back to awareness and adjustments to find balance. (Recall the bicycle and Einstein!)

13) How do I recover from a pressure-filled day?

Each person will recover differently. Some people can do it on the commute home, perhaps listening to an audiobook.

Others need to go to the gym. Others might need to read or just "veg in front of the TV" to renew themselves. I prefer just a few minutes of silence. (Recall the value of silence as an antidote to pressure in the "Seeking Equilibrium" chapter.)

14) **What is the best trick/tool/technique I can use to make pressure work for me instead of against me?**

By applying and using the **3 P's** and understanding the traits required in any peak performance: **Confidence**, **Relaxation** and **Focus**. (See chapters on "Relax" & "3 P's.")

15) **How can I re-center or re-focus my mind when I slip back into the "pressure is bad" school of thought?**

I would recommend that you re-read the Introduction, "Pressure in a Different Light," and ask yourself, "How can I best 'refract' this pressure? What is the vision, ideal end-state, goal or outcome?" Then remind yourself that the pressure wants to be "fuel" to help you get there.

16) **What about choking? I read this entire book and you didn't mention choking once.**

Peyton Manning's quote touched on it, though. People tend to choke "when they don't know what the hell they are doing," or they are over-thinking and hyper-self-aware. Choking is most often the result of not appropriately planning, preparing and practicing. Many people think they are prepared, and maybe they are, but they haven't practiced properly – they haven't become habituated. All these ideas are reviewed in the chapters "Relax" and "3 P's." While they cannot guarantee a peak performance, they do guarantee your best *opportunity* to experience a peak performance.

17) **Doesn't positive peer pressure actually facilitate goal achievement?**

> Very few things are stronger than an aligned and unified team under pressure, particularly if it is competing against another team. While any team is only as good as its weakest link, positive peer pressure strengthens each member – inspiring even the weakest members to improve and become better. "For the strength of the pack is the wolf, and the strength of the wolf is the pack."[58] Recall the "SEAL for a Day" chapter and the EO story of positive peer pressure.

18) **I golf a lot, and I've heard that older golfers tend to get the putting yips (choke) under pressure more often because they have a lifetime of missed putts in their memory banks, whereas a younger golfer has no such inventory. So, how would the person who has a history of underperforming under pressure (choking) erase those memories? He can change his future behavior, but those memories are there.**

> One of the great adages in ALL of sports is to "have a short memory" – the ability to forget quickly what just went wrong and immediately reapply your focus to the moment and what needs to happen! Developing a short memory is critical to success. Try to recall Ben Hogan's great quote, "The most important shot in golf is the next one." It's a "next" mentality – the next opportunity for greatness is on the way. There is no past, there is no future...there is NOW, and now is where the concentration and focus need to be applied. What's done is done.

19) **David Bowie sang "Pressure, pushing down on me, pressing down on you, no man ask for." Are we wired to avoid pressure, or are past failures keeping us from "asking" for pressure?**

Recalling Freud's "pleasure principle," you will notice there is definitely an element that has us wired and preconditioned to avoid pain (pressure); P.A.M., the pain avoidance mechanism, wants to have her way. However, the "greats" find a way to use their past failures as fuel. Please revisit the "Chip on the Shoulder" section and "The Most Productive Day of the Year."

20) **How can we tell which employees will respond well when pressure is applied to them to increase their productivity? Is it up to us, the employer, to hire with this trait in mind, or are we supposed to develop it for the employee?**

I think it's a great question; many business owners will outright ask prospective employees, "How do you handle pressure?" Some candidates are taught to say, "I "thrive under pressure," so that should beget a further analysis: "What do you think of pressure? Is it good or bad?" Since change is a constant and change is a form of pressure, it is ideal to have employees who welcome change/pressure and view it as an opportunity for growth for themselves and the company.

21) **What is a good plan of action in the heat of the moment when the pressure seems to be too much?**

Feel your feet on the ground – awaken to your senses, so to speak, and breathe. Take deep breaths. This helps you stay grounded vs. "flighty," and helps to bring your attention to the present moment. "Lose yourself" by putting your attention and focus on the mission, outcome and message, not yourself. This is detailed in the "RELAX" chapter, and the idea is not to be too self-aware or overly self-conscious.

BONUS – GIFTS PAGE

Bonus 1: Free Pressure <u>PRISM Assessment</u>*

Expected availability December 2015

Bonus 2: <u>Free 28 Days, The Habit Factor ProCloud Web</u>*

*   *Currently <u>iOS only</u> (beta)*

NOTE:: Email Subject: **"CloudPro PROMO"** to: sales (AT) equilibrium-ent.com for promo code

Bonus 3: <u>Free Audiobook Chapters</u>*

When available, expected by December 2015!

<u>**Subscribe**</u> to Martin's top-ranked "**Habits 2 Goals**" Podcast: <u>iTunes</u> or <u>Android</u>.

Peak Performance Tip Sheet

◆ **Welcome the pressure.** *Recognize it's a test that you are worthy and capable of passing. (Don't resist it!)*

◆ **Reaffirm** *your Purpose & Mission. Know your WHY.*

◆ **Plan, Prepare & Practice** *(Revisit the "3 P's" Chapter.)*

◆ **Practice. Practice. Practice** *– "Practice puts brains in your muscles." Habits operate with limited to no conscious thought.* **Routines and habits** *are developed through intentional practice and repetition and forge relaxation.*[ee]

◆ **"Lose Yourself"** *– Focus on the message, not yourself!*

◆ **To be loose and relaxed** *(snap fingers, sing song in head)!*

◆ **Focus** *on the upside – Focus on the positive outcome!*

◆ **Meditate** *to help relax and visualize outcome.*

◆ **Minimize** *failure. It will not be fatal! (Hopefully ;)*

◆ **Conduct a "pre-mortem."** *Can you guess what will go wrong? What can be done to avoid it?*

◆ **Concentrate:** *Gather knowledge and available best practices and strategies.*

◆ **Recall** *past "winning" physiological emotions and states.*

◆ **Know the "Zone"** *qualities of Peak Performance. What's your anchor?*

◆ **Let GO of the outcome** *and just P.L.A.Y! ("Relax" Chapter)*

◆ **Feel your feet!** *(Stay grounded.) Breathe deeply.*

◆ **Focus** *on the "controllables."*

[ee] http://www.buzzfeed.com/lizlanteri/top-10-rituals-and-trademarks-by-famous-tv-hosts-63hh#.sk80JXXP3

ACKNOWLEDGEMENTS

*"There are two great days in your life: the day
you're born and the day you find out why."*
~Mark Twain

I feel compelled to share that I did *not*, contrary to best practices in the publishing industry, cleverly sample book titles or even subtitles, nor did I do *any* market research on any of this book's content. Instead, I chose to write a book I *wished I read 20 years ago.*

I truly wish someone had given me these two books (*The Habit Factor* and *The Pressure Paradox*) – although, to be honest, I'm not sure I would have been smart enough to read them back then. Many of you who've known me for that long can testify to the truth in that statement.

In both instances – first with *The Habit Factor* and now with *The Pressure Paradox* – it's become clear that I'm simply trying to solve and work through my own challenges as they arise, and in the process I have recognized the value in sharing these ideas and my corresponding results with others. "Teach once and learn twice," Dr. Stephen Covey used to say. Although that awareness makes this somewhat of a selfish act, I do hope thousands and ultimately millions of people will read these books. But even if nobody ever read them, I have no doubt that I would still be far better for the effort.

There is no way I could ever write these books without the many talented, fascinating and creative individuals who've guided me (either directly or indirectly) along the way.

The fact that time cannot be saved is just another reason why it is so much more precious than money. Then again, in a strange way, by writing and sharing our thoughts, we can sort of pause time or maybe just slow it down a little.

There have been so many great thinkers and authors who've taken the time to record their ideas, and I'm immensely grateful for their insight and dedication. For many of them, I suspect the same might be true – that they too were working through their own personal challenges when crafting their works.

There are far too many authors and influencers to recount here; however, I'm determined to make an attempt. First, to the late, great Dr. Wayne Dyer (I thought for sure we'd be hanging out in Maui); to Brian Tracy (referenced probably a dozen times throughout this work), a prolific living legend who continues to provide incredible support and guidance; to Tony Robbins, Dr. Stephen Covey, Napoleon Hill, Norman Vincent Peale, Warren S. Rustand, Michael Gerber, John Assaraf, Holly Green, Verne Harnish, Darren Hardy, Tony Smith, Jack Daly, Gary Ridge, Michael Gerber and Chip Conley.

To the philosophical masters who've made writing and learning enjoyable: Lao Tzu, Confucius, Aristotle, Socrates, Marcus Aurelius, Henry David Thoreau, Ralph Waldo Emerson, Seneca, Alan Watts and Jim Rohn (to name a small handful). To the American greats cited herein: Benjamin Franklin (the great-grandfather of personal development), Thomas Jefferson, Abraham Lincoln, George Washington and MLK.

Collectively, I know these authors and thinkers have likely saved me from myself countless times.

And that may be the perfect segue, as I'll bring this a little closer to home.

First, **MOM!** Early on, you always provided me a vision and ideal to look up to – to grow up to. Today, you are as consistently creative and inspiring as you were in my earliest memories. I know my effort here is laced with your creativity!

Dad! If you're not the smartest guy on the planet, I'm not sure who is (perhaps it's Bapop!). Either way, you and Mom have always provided the perfect harmony (even in rough times) of yin and yang. Similarly, your intellect has undoubtedly shaped many of these ideas. You always encouraged me to think constructively and counterintuitively. I recall as a teacher you were a master of pressure, particularly when it came to teaching me subjects like math and even chess – always *asking* questions, challenging me, and insisting that I keep searching for the answers.

To my very special partners: Edmon, Christine, Duke and Colleen. (Colleen, you will never be forgotten. You were as beautiful as you were creative. We all miss you dearly!) Edmon, I continue to say to anyone who'll listen that I'm fortunate to work with one of the world's great mentors, and by the way, it was you who planted the seed early on for this book. Duke, I've always subscribed to the idea that a partnership is best in threes, and it appears that the founding fathers agreed – it just so happens that a triangle is the strongest of geometric shapes. Duke, you have made this a great and powerful partnership!

To the Linghams, all of you! I said it in THF and I'll say it here: What were you thinking!? Bapop and Nanny, your support for all things (particularly kid related) has helped beyond imagination. It truly takes a village. To Grandma Margaret and Uncle Sean, you are sorely missed but never forgotten.

ACKNOWLEDGEMENTS

To the "Bro-in law" – you'd be hard-pressed to find a more successful man. From busboy to business owner, I can't wait to read *your* book! Many years ago we discussed some of these ideas and you shared the following: "Why can't every day be like the day before vacation? It's the most productive day of the year!" Yes – that is a chapter title!

My amazing brothers Richard, Anders and the "little" bro Mark! Life is a fantastic journey with you guys by my side (near and far). To Lisa & Denise and the amazing nieces and nephews; Lindsey and Lily and Luke, Noah and Julius.

To the scores of incredible personal and corporate sponsors of MG and The Habit Factor (in no particular order): SENTRE Partners (Williams & Spathas and Co.), Bird Rock Systems, Zenzi, College Works, Dolce & Pane, Signature Furniture Rental, Entrepreneurs Organization, Vistage (Mr. Chalmers), TEDx Al Ain, San Diego Professional Coaches Alliance, Sales Leadership Alliance, Southwest Realtors Association, NAI, JMS/SPAWAR, U.S. Green Chamber, EO Accelerator. To my Accelerator groups (past and present), EOFace: Tia, Neil, Megan, Tara, Erica, Will, Matt; Beau & Crush: Henry, Mike, David, Austin (thanks for the launch insight!), Ajay, & Jennifer. I can't mention EO without thanking The ROCK: Brendan, Jon, Casey, Sarah, Paul, Moaddeli, Ortiz, Owen, Sergio, Jennifer and Mr. Berman as well as ex-members Derek, Wayne, Hoffy, Scotty, David, Shaun and Reid.

To the people who tend to recommend and promote The Habit Factor even in my absence – the greatest sponsors and friends you could hope for: Christopher Payne (two brilliant videos!), Jim Matteo, Bing Bush, Jeff Becker, John Barrett, Brett Stapper, Brandon Stapper, Gregor Shanks, JC Ripper, John Lingham, Martha Cullimore, T. Greenwood, Ian O'roarty, Jordan Ramos, Casey Wright, Shane Whaley, Alex Shahabe, Tim Hawbolt, and Bryan Wright. Additional thanks to the launch team contributors for their insight and support: Lance, Evan, Jeff Becker, John Barrett, April, Boren, Susan, Lingham, Fasbinder, and Papa Allen.

To the great indie supporters of The Habit Factor portal who bought into The Pressure Paradox nearly two years before it came out: Bennett Fisher (we call him Coach!), Casey Wright, Rory McLaughlin (Rory, how many times did the deadline for this project move?), and Jon Carder (big wave surfer!).

Other supporters who helped to keep me pumped about these ideas (in no particular order): Mike Smith, Drew Goodmanson, David Brott, Sean Boren, Nick Norris, Bennett Fisher, Matt Garrett, Fred Gaston, Rick Valentine, Gregg Fasbinder, Eric Kauffman, Jeremy Pound, Jesse Patton, Casey Wright, Tim Ortiz, Michel Kripalani, Sam Mehta, Scott Krawitz, Noemi Kis, Kevin Espiritu, Chuck Longanecker, Harrell, McDaniel Julien B., Metzler, Popovic, Mr. Mendell, Sue Hesse, K. Potashner, Rick V. Walt C., Donna Maria, Shane

Whaley, Ms. Ganus, JD Herrerah, Jeremy Pound, John Cocozza, the Lavers (Rod, Rick & Sue), Nanci & Greg, John & Mary, Brian & Josie and G-Man. Hey, G-Man! I'm writing a book and this time I think you know about it.

More great coaches and authors who've collaborated and/or supported along the way: Christopher Payne, Eric Kauffman, Rich Phillips, Timi Gleason, Rick Sessinghaus, Michael Anderson, Heidi Hanna, Mike Koenigs, Sue Hesse, Jack Daly, Ken Schmitt, Jennie Brown, Brian Traichel Hal Elrod, Jairek Robbins and Angela Martin. To the Podcasters: Nick Palkowski, KFM and OAC; Andrew Ferebee, Jordan and Jason of The Art of Charm fame.

To THE Band: Fink, Fleming and Ognall – *living* legends (let's see how long we can keep it that way).

To my best men *again*: Levy, Hodge, RG and Laden-hosen.

To the masterful IT team at C3 Networx! If you guys weren't so great, this wouldn't be possible.

Finally, Papa Allen and your beautiful family (Marie-Line, Kellie & Bryce) your brilliance helped spark this – you willingly wrote (and recorded) the foreword, and you have a chapter named after you. You helped me crystalize so many of these ideas and concepts, occasionally over a nicely chilled Rye. THANK YOU my brother!

Gretchen! It must get old hearing my praise of you – you are the sage and the saint who makes it all possible and your kids are pretty amazing too. Hey, let's do a couple more books Okay? LOVE YOU! To everyone else THANK YOU very much! ;)

Screenshot: MG puts The Habit Factor® (app) to good use (again) and finishes another goal: "Complete *The Pressure Paradox*".

A Short List of Paradoxes

- This page intentionally left blank.
- You are totally and completely unique and special, just like everyone else.
- Real knowledge is knowing the extent of one's ignorance.
- The best time to relax is when you don't have the time.
- Expect to be surprised, and if you are not surprised, then you will be surprised!
- I shut my eyes in order to see.
- If we were happy all the time we'd be miserable.
- I would have written a shorter letter but I did not have the time.
- Time: You can spend it but not own it. It is priceless yet it is free.
- Without illusion there can be no enlightenment. ~Buddha
- Failure is the foundation of success, and the means by which it is achieved. Success is the lurking place for failure.
- Everything is subjective, and that is an objective statement.
- This statement is false.
- Change is one of the great constants in life.

How do you *respond* when the pressure's on?

How do you respond when the pressure's on?
When the chance for victory is almost gone.
When Fortune's star has refused to shine,
When the ball is on your five yard line?

How do you respond when the going's rough?

Does your spirit lag when the breaks are tough?
Or, is there in you a flame that glows brighter as
fiercer the battle grows?

How hard, how long will you fight that foe?
That's what the world would like to know!

Cowards can fight when they're out ahead.
It's the uphill grind that reveals the thoroughbred!

You wish for success, isn't that so?
Then tell me son, how will you respond when the
pressure's on? ff

~Unknown

---

ff "Respond" replaces the word "act" from the original version of the poem.

AUTHOR BIO

Martin Grunburg is the creator/inventor of The Habit Factor® app as well as the author of the international bestselling book sharing the same name. He's widely regarded as the father of the modern habit-tracking movement, originally publishing The Habit Factor app in 2009, which at the time was the first to provide a unique and simplified goal-achievement methodology *specifically via positive habit development and alignment.*

Martin presented these revolutionary insights about habit and goal achievement at TEDx in the United Arab Emirates in 2010, and his work has been featured in the world's most popular productivity blogs such as Lifehacker.com and Mashable.com, as well as The New York Times, C|Net and OpenForum. He's been identified by Success Magazine as one of today's most inspirational, creative and respected thought-leaders in the multibillion-dollar personal-development arena.

Martin is currently a partner in C3 Networx, formerly Home2Office Computing Solutions, Inc. As founder/COO, he's been nominated twice for the Entrepreneur of the Year award and has twice led his team to win the Better Business Bureau Torch Award for Marketplace Ethics.

Martin serves on the board of Big Brothers Big Sisters regionally in San Diego and became a "Big Brother" more than 15 years ago. He currently serves on the Entrepreneurs Organization (San Diego) board as the Mentor Chair. Prior to that, he has served as volunteer instructor for Junior Achievement, teaching "Success Skills" to some of the city's more economically challenged high schools.

Martin is an avid waterman, surfer and sailor who has completed the Catalina Classic (a 32-mile open-ocean paddle) multiple times and considers himself an "accidental triathlete," having completed several full Ironman-distance triathlons (one in France).

Martin resides in Pacific Beach, California with his wife and two daughters.

Join Martin and catch up with his latest endeavors, **SUBSCRIBE** to his top-ranked **"Habits 2 Goals"** **Podcast** in iTunes or Android.

Coaches: If you're interested in connecting and becoming certified in The Habit Factor® and now The Pressure Paradox™ methodologies for your clients, please visit: http://directory.thehabitfactor.com.

Readers: Please **share** your Habit Factor, and now Pressure Paradox, success stories by emailing: success (at) thehabitfactor.com.

For updates on Martin's coaching programs and to contact him for speaking appearances, please visit: http://thehabitfactor.com/meet-martin.

THE PRESSURE PARADOX

NOTES

THE PRESSURE PARADOX

NOTES

End Notes:

Bibliography and Additional References

[1] http://faculty.washington.edu/jdb/345/345%20Articles/Baumeister%20et%20 0al.%20%281998%29.pdf

[2] http://en.wikipedia.org/wiki/Broken_windows_theory

[3] http://www.foxnews.com/health/2012/06/08/cdc-teen-suicide-attempts-on-rise/

[4] http://www.scientificamerican.com/article/short-term-stress-boosts-immune-systems/

[5] https://en.wikipedia.org/wiki/Visible_spectrum -

[6] https://en.wikipedia.org/wiki/Refraction

[7] https://en.wikipedia.org/wiki/The_Chicken_and_the_Pig

[8] http://www.apa.org/monitor/feb08/oxytocin.aspx

[9] *Performing Under Pressure*, Page 28, shares contradictory information regarding time pressure and resultant creativity.

[10] YouTube video interview: https://www.youtube.com/watch?v=_FqZkU1Fjd8 (min 8:40)

[11] SQL query supplied by Joe at: http://killersports.com. BTW: Fourth quarter scoring in NBA over 20 years is 24.61% (1995-2014).

[12] http://darrenhardy.success.com/2011/02/get-in-the-game/

[13] http://www.consumeraffairs.com/news/att-fined-100-million-for-throttling-unlimited-data-connections-061715.html

[14] http://www.amnh.org/exhibitions/past-exhibitions/brain-the-inside-story/your-emotional-brain/beyond-our-lizard-brain/

[15] Thanks to Ryan Holiday, author of *The Obstacle is the Way*, for guiding me to this passage!

[16]https://en.wikipedia.org/wiki/Spanish_conquest_of_the_Aztec_Empire

[17] https://en.wikipedia.org/wiki/Xin_(concept)

[18] http://www.nytimes.com/2012/07/29/sunday-review/why-olympic-records-are-broken-or-not.html?_r=0

[19] http://www.foxsports.com/buzzer/story/chip-on-his-shoulder-epidemic-causes-diagnosis-treatment-092314

[20] http://www.ysr1560.com/john-granato/russell-wilson-playing-with-a-chip-on-his-shoulder-8407/

[21] http://www.nydailynews.com/sports/football/seahawks-carry-chip-shoulder-super-bowl-article-1.1595958
Great video: Deaf, Derrick Coleman with something to prove!:
https://www.youtube.com/watch?v=JzQFA2hxyRQ

[22] http://articles.baltimoresun.com/2011-05-18/entertainment/bs-sm-oprahs-baltimore-20110522_1_oprah-winfrey-show-baltimore-history-wjz/2

[23] http://www.nps.gov/edis/faqs.htm

[24]http://www.sandiegouniontribune.com/news/2014/mar/23/bigbang-universe-scientists/

[25] http://www.nj.com/soccer-news/index.ssf/2015/07/womens_world_cup_carli_lloyd.html

[26]http://www.slate.com/blogs/the_spot/2015/07/03/usa_v_japan_preview_carli_lloyd_morgan_brian_and_lauren_holiday_describe.html

[27] https://en.wikipedia.org/wiki/Lose_Yourself

[28] http://sanfrancisco.suntimes.com/golden-state-warriors/7/74/134498/stephen-curry-mvp-reactions

http://www.knbr.com/2015/04/09/curry-makes-mvp-statement-in-spellbinding-performance/

[29]https://www.facebook.com/TonyRobbins/posts/10150839953954060

[30] https://en.wikipedia.org/wiki/Habituation

END NOTES

[31] http://www.drweil.com/drw/u/ART00521/three-breathing-exercises.html

[32] https://www.stephencovey.com/mission-statements.php

[33] http://freakonomics.com/2014/06/05/failure-is-your-friend-a-new-freakonomics-radio-podcast/

[34] http://www.telegraph.co.uk/news/uknews/1575348/How-Edmund-Hillary-conquered-Everest.html

http://www.siredmundhillary.com/hillary.htm

[35] https://en.wikipedia.org/wiki/Rod_Laver

[36] https://www.youtube.com/watch?v=llNuwhZWXKA

[37] https://en.wikipedia.org/wiki/Floyd_Mayweather,_Jr.

[38] http://www.wsj.com/articles/SB10001424052970203986604577257420695000272

[39] http://www.washingtonpost.com/sports/othersports/tennis/2012/07/06/gJQA4eK1RW_story.html

[40] https://www.gazelles.com/static/resources/articles/Coaching.pdf

[41] https://en.wikipedia.org/wiki/Kelley_O%27Hara

[42] http://www.mercenarytrader.com/2012/09/how-jerry-rice-achieved-greatness/

[43] http://www.bigstory.ap.org/article/manning-plays-football-chess-masters-mind

[44] https://en.wikipedia.org/wiki/K%C3%BCbler-Ross_model

[45] Wentworth Upham, George, *The Life of General Washington: First President of the United States, Volume 1.* HardPress Publishing, January 2012.

[46] Lane, Jason, *General and Madame de Lafayette: Partners in Liberty's Cause in the American and French Revolutions,* Taylor Trade Publishing, October 2003.

[47] Copeland, Lewis; Lamm, Lawrence W.; McKenna, Stephen J; *The World's Great Speeches: Fourth Enlarged (1999) Edition,* Dover Publications, September 1999.

[48] https://sites.sas.upenn.edu/duckworth

[49] http://www.ted.com/talks/angela_lee_duckworth_the_key_to_success_grit?language=en

[50] https://en.wikipedia.org/wiki/A_Boy_Named_Sue

[51] http://www.pbs.org/wgbh/nova/physics/theory-behind-equation.html

[52] https://en.wikipedia.org/wiki/Division_by_zero
https://en.wikipedia.org/wiki/Infinity

[53] http://www.dailymail.co.uk/news/article-2275735/The-letter-changed-Indian-history-Gandhi-s-prison-plea-freedom-important-EVER-ll-cost-15-000-auction.html

[54] https://en.wikipedia.org/wiki/Letter_from_Birmingham_Jail

[55] http://www.lionsroar.com/mandelas-key/

[56] http://theartofcharm.com/podcast-episodes/dan-millman-the-way-of-the-peaceful-warrior/

[57] http://www.nytimes.com/2005/08/02/science/your-body-is-younger-than-you-think.html?_r=0

[58] Law of the Jungle https://en.wikipedia.org/wiki/Law_of_the_jungle

Made in the USA
Charleston, SC
03 November 2015